Doctor to the Mouse

Updated Stories from a Walt Disney World Physician

Anthony M. Rizzo, M.D.

Deltaville, VA

ISBN: 978-1-962935-74-6

First Edition: April 2026

Published by: High Tide Publications, Inc.
www.Hightidepublications.com

Disclaimer

This book is a memoir. It reflects the author's present recollections of experiences over time. Some names and identifying details have been changed to protect the privacy of individuals. Some events have been compressed, and some dialogue has been recreated for narrative clarity.

Library of Congress Cataloging-in-Publication Data
Names: Rizzo, Anthony, author.
Title: Doctor to the Mouse: Updated Stories from a Walt Disney World Physician / Anthony M. Rizzo, M.D.
Description: Deltaville, Virginia : High Tide Publications, Inc., 2026.
Identifiers: 978-1-962935-74-6* ISBN: (paperback)

Contents

To my wife,
children,
children-in-law,
and
grandchildren

You'll be in my heart, always.

Introduction

Peter Pan walked into Magic Kingdom First Aid holding his forearms in an unusual manner. His smile was more of a grimace. His boyfriend hotfooted it by his side.

"Fuck, fuck, fuck!" was all Peter Pan had to say.

It was obvious he had broken both of his forearms.

When I asked him how it happened, all he would say was, "Fuck, fuck, fuck!"

His boyfriend was a little more forthcoming. Peter had been on the riverboat *Liberty Belle*. At the time, the boat was being used for character meet-and-greets. As many costume characters as possible walked about the boat interacting with guests. There were characters in fur as well as face characters.

Side note: Any character in a costume that includes a head, such as Mickey or Minnie Mouse, is called "being in fur." Any character that does not wear a head, such as Belle, is called a "face character."

Peter Pan was a face character who had fallen downstairs from the top deck to the deck below landing on his outstretched forearms. It looked like he had managed to break the radius and ulna of both forearms, giving himself bilateral Colles' fractures.

He had had to finish the riverboat's circuit, then, after the boat docked and the guests disembarked, he had walked through the park to First Aid while maintaining character. Hence the grimacing smile.

The trouble was cast member First Aid and guest First Aid were connected, and guests could easily hear Peter Pan's constant stream of expletives.

So, now there were a few problems. First, how was I to get Peter Pan to shut up? Second, how was I to deal with the guests, just down the hall, who were continuing to hear Peter's tirade? Third, how was I to get Peter Pan to hold still for X-rays? Fourth, how was I to get Peter Pan out of costume and into his own clothes to send him to an orthopedist? Peter Pan's clothes were in a locker in the tunnel somewhere.

I managed to get the films, and, sure enough, Peter Pan had four fractured forearm bones—bilateral Colles' fractures. I splinted both of his forearms. I sent his boyfriend for his clothes then called a friend who was an orthopedist specializing in the hand.

"Rich, this is Tony. I've got Peter Pan here with bilateral Colles' fractures. ... Yup, fell down a flight of stairs on the *Liberty Belle* landing on outstretched hands. … Okay, I'll send him with his films to your office."

Peter Pan's problems were just beginning. How was he to eat, toilet, dress, and generally take care of himself with both forearms in casts?

How did I get myself into this crazy position?

How Did I Get Myself into this Crazy Position?

I was an active duty surgeon in the United States Air Force, stationed at the Air Force Academy in Colorado Springs, Colorado. Mine was a major Disneyphile family. In my spare time, I had been writing a trivia book about all things Disney, and, while doing the research, I found out about the yet-to-be-announced Celebration Project.

I wondered what the Celebration Project was, so I made some calls. It didn't take long to find Charles Adams.

Charles Adams was heading the Celebration Project, and he was very approachable on the phone. When I told him about myself and my book, he invited me to stop by if I was ever in Central Florida.

Never a family that needed much of an excuse to visit Walt Disney World, we immediately planned a trip. One afternoon, while the kids and my wife were in the Magic Kingdom, I met with Charles.

We had a long, involved discussion. The upshot of the meeting was Charles asking me if I would be willing to "answer a few questions from time to time" involving Celebration planning.

Of course I agreed.

Soon after we returned to the Air Force Academy, I received a thick, 8 ½ x 11-inch envelope from Charles. It contained page after page of tentative plans for Celebration. Charles asked me to comment on each of them. It was a pretty big task!

I ended up sending lengthy responses, sometimes twenty pages, in answer to a single question.

The first envelope was followed by another, then another, then another. For each, I spent hours answering questions and giving suggestions.

One evening, Charles called and said, "Tony, we want you to come down and work with us on the Celebration Project." My answer was that, as much as it was an honor, I was on active duty and loved my service in the USAF.

Charles persisted. He stated that Disney had partnered with what was then Florida Hospital in Orlando (now Advent Health) to build the Celebration Hospital. Charles told me he could arrange for me to become a faculty member in the residency, teaching surgery to family practice interns and residents. Charles sweetened the pot when he said he could guarantee me a home site in Celebration.

I had nine years of active duty under my belt and needed another eleven to be able to retire. My retirement plan had been to find a residency in which I could teach surgery. My family always wanted to live in Central Florida.

Here was my retirement plan being offered to me eleven years early!

The problem was that I really loved the Air Force and what I was doing.

My wife and I spent several days thinking and discussing and finally hit upon a solution. The Florida Air National Guard flew F-16s and needed a flight surgeon. I could move from active duty to the Guard, take the position at Florida Hospital, teach surgery, work with Charles Adams on Celebration, and still serve in the Air Force.

So that's what we did.

But, unlike Disney fairytales, the happily-ever-after part was a little tarnished.

The Guard unit, at that time, was in shambles. After one year, I moved from the Guard to the USAF Reserve and was soon commanding a squadron at Patrick Air Force Base.

Florida Hospital only wanted me in order to pressure some of the surgical private practices to sell to them, causing the surgeons to become Florida Hospital employees.

Florida Hospital wanted to design the Celebration Hospital to be a pseudo-religious facility and, when I stated that was not my opinion of the right way to design a medical facility, I was excluded from all future meetings.

Disney decided that any promises made to people about home sites in Celebration were null and void—see the chapter on Celebration. Instead, Disney decided to have a lottery for eighty single-family sites and a number of multiple-family dwellings. Charles was at least sorry when I pointed out I had uprooted my family and changed my entire life for an empty promise.

On the plus side, my family was chosen to be one of the original eighty families in Celebration. Was the lottery rigged? I'll never know.

And, because I was teaching in the residency, I got an unexpected introduction to Walt Disney World.

The medical staff at WDW consisted of three full-time doctors, all of whom had trained in the residency where I was teaching. All were recent graduates. They worked Monday through Friday, but WDW required doctors to be in place seven days per week for potential occupational injuries.

Our residents worked part time at WDW as weekend docs. But, because they were residents with on-call responsibilities, frequently they could not make their scheduled shifts. As I had administrative responsibility for assigning the residents to the weekend position, I was soon called upon to work a few shifts.

Soon I was regularly scheduled instead of just filling in from time to time. At that point, I became what Disney at that time called a CT—Casual Temporary—cast member.

CTs normally did not accrue retirement or other benefits. However, WDW had a special category for physician CTs. The result was that, although I was a weekend doc, I was considered full time at WDW as far as benefits were concerned, to include accruing retirement and having free passes to the parks.

I was in hog heaven.

Coincident with my discovery that Florida Hospital had me on faculty only to pressure the community surgeons to sell their practices—something abhorrent to me—a fulltime position at WDW opened up, and I was offered the job.

So, I left teaching surgery to do fulltime occupational medicine at Walt Disney World. The decision to leave surgery, the specialty I loved and trained for all of those years, was made easier by the concurrent news of a medical diagnosis in a close loved one. That diagnosis would require me to have regular working hours, something surgery would never have allowed.

I started at what was then Disney/MGM Studios, then worked at EPCOT, then Magic Kingdom, and finally at Central Health Services when that opened.

At one point, I went back to weekends, from full time, to work weekdays initiating a new service to guests. The service provided house calls to their resort rooms, again under the auspices of Florida Hospital.

My time with WDW ended with the 9/11 terrorist attacks, when I immediately returned to active duty in the USAF and remained on active duty until my Air Force retirement in 2013.

This is the story of each of those Disney phases.

A Note on Name Tags:

> WDW did not want guests to know that company doctors were on property. Disney Docs were for cast members only. Our job was occupational health.

Every cast member is called by his/her first name, so cast member's name tags had first names. This tradition started with a name tag with the name WALT on it.

The exception was the Docs. My name tag said DR. RIZZO. But I was not, ever, ever to wear that name tag onstage where guests could read it. Disney did not want injured or ill guests to demand to see the doctor, as the company did not want the legal responsibility. Regardless of the severity of a guest's illness or injury, Reedy Creek Fire and Rescue was called and the guest was transported off property ASAP. Disney Docs never saw guests. Period. I had a second name tag that said TONY for times I had to go onstage.

2

Becoming a Disney Executive

WDW considered the Disney Docs to be company executives. As such, I was assigned to a two-week training course on how to be a Disney exec.

There were some real eye-openers during those two weeks. Here are a few examples:

The lawyer who spoke to us talked about the many daily lawsuits WDW faces. That is discussed elsewhere in this book.

The resorts were represented by the general manager of the Contemporary Hotel. His big take-away for me was the scale of his enterprise. In response to a question about resort profit margins, he stated he could not understand how a hotel or resort with "only a few rooms" ever made any money. The Contemporary has approximately 750 rooms. By "only a few rooms" he was referring to places with less than 150 rooms!

The merchandise presenter talked about Disney's merchandise profit margins. He stated that Disney charged "double plus 10%." That meant that if Disney procured an item for $1.00, they would charge $2.20 for it. My level of cast member received 35% off when we purchased merchandise items. So, if I decided to buy the $2.20 item, I would pay $1.43. Since Disney acquired the item for $1.00, the company still made a 43% profit.

Very rarely, Disney would sell an item for 50% off. The $2.20 item would sell for $1.10. Still a 10% profit. When you consider that conventional grocery store chains have an average profit margin of about 2.2%, Disney is doing pretty well. (see https://thegrocerystoreguy.com/what-is-the-profit-margin-for-grocery-stores)

As a Disney Exec, I received a sticker for my windshield that gave me access to every part of the property. At the time, pre-9/11, security booths protected only backstage areas. Since I came and went so often to the backstage areas of every part of the property, I got to know the assigned security officers quite well. One of them even gave me gifts! I mention it because whenever I brought my family to the parks, I parked backstage and walked my family onstage for the visit. We had unlimited free access to the parks, so I was not sneaking my family in—I was simply bypassing the guest parking lots and the entry lines. Actually, this was pretty much standard procedure for other execs as well.

For Kingdom, we parked directly behind the east side of Main Street, U.S.A. We walked in via the cast access next to Tony's Town Square Restaurant. The reason we did not park behind the west side of Main Street, U.S.A, by First Aid, was that the 3:00 parade ended there, and the night parade was staged there. It was possible to be trapped by a parade on the west side.

At EPCOT, we parked behind the American Adventure and accessed the park there.

At Studios we parked on the west side of Sunset Boulevard, near costuming, and accessed the park next to Rosie's All American Café. This entrance directly faced Beauty and the Beast Live On Stage.

One day, my youngest daughter told me she was talking to her grade school classmates about going to Disney. She said she could not understand why her classmates didn't enter Studios through "the Beauty and the Beast gate." She told me her friends described huge parking lots, taking trams, the Monorail, or boats (in the case of Kingdom). Her friends described how long it took to get from the car to the gates, and how long they had to wait to get through the gates. It had never dawned on me that my kids had never been in a Disney guest parking lot! And, being little kids, they thought what we did to go to the parks was standard for everyone.

Referring to the parking stickers, one of the Kingdom nurses dearly wanted the parking access the Docs had. He wanted it so much he decided to counterfeit a sticker for himself.

Unfortunately for him, Security made regular rounds and checked that parking assignments were being followed. When Security checked Kingdom First Aid's few spots, he ran the number on each of our stickers. The nurse's sticker number did not compute! When confronted, the nurse admitted to counterfeiting the sticker. A multi-year exemplary employee, except for sticker-envy, the nurse was terminated on the spot and escorted from the property.

3

The Universal Bogeyman

One day, I got called away from seeing patients to attend an all-executive and all-management meeting to be held in a huge convention space in the Contemporary Hotel. I had never received such a summons and wondered what to expect.

A vice-president stood at the podium and read a guest satisfaction letter. It praised the resort, singling the ride that went up and down with the terrifying drops. It loved the character meet-and-greets. It gushed about the on-property resort and the cast members who worked there. It applauded the variety of restaurants and the quality of the food.

It was written for Universal Studios.

This was a meeting about fear.

Universal was expanding, had added a second park, was opening on-property resorts, and was stealing WDW cast members and making them Universal team members.

This was a meeting admonishing everyone in the room to get their cast members to work even harder than they were working to try to keep Disney Number One among theme parks.

I have no idea if this scare tactic worked, but I cannot help but notice WDW is still here and seems to be doing fine.

Doing Disney Jobs

In order to fully understand the rigors flight crews undergo, U.S. Air Force flight surgeons are rated in their squadron's aircraft. That means that USAF aerospace medicine physicians regularly fly missions in the aircraft.

When I became a full-time Disney Doc, I brought that philosophy with me. I wanted to perform as many of the jobs as possible, so I would understand the mechanisms of the injuries I had been seeing as a weekend Doc. As a full-timer, I hoped to prevent some injuries by understanding the cast positions.

That said, I was the only one of the four full-time Disney Docs at with this philosophy when I was a full-time cast member. The other docs made it clear they wanted nothing to do with going across property to understand the other cast jobs. In fact, one of them rarely, if ever, visited the parks at all as a guest!

Voyage of the Little Mermaid

Voyage of the Little Mermaid fascinated me. There was an onstage quick change when Ariel lost her fins and got legs. Max, the dog, had a costume that required a cast member to walk on all fours. The puppetry was amazing. I wanted to know how all of it was done.

I approached the show's management and asked to be involved in a day of performance.

They allowed me to be backstage for the puppetry part of a performance, and it really is ingenious how costuming and lighting create magic for the guests in the audience.

I asked to be shown the fin-to-leg change, including having it done to me. They obliged.

Ariel normally sits on a rock, her legs inserted into the fin so she can flex and extend the fin during her performance.

The fin has a steel cord attached to its top. The other end of the cord is attached to a powerful, quick-acting winch. When the change from fin to legs is to occur, Ariel is standing on the rock, not holding on to anything and not secured in any way, when the winch quickly pulls the fin down from her waist into the rock, revealing Ariel's dress and her human legs.

It's quite an experience! I felt as if I was going to be pulled down from the rock when the winch activated. The 100-pound actresses who withstood that for multiple shows per day were incredible.

I actually hate to admit what I did to find out how the dog costume worked. On a different day from when I wore Ariel's fin, and without first discussing it with show's management, I talked with one of the cast members who worked the Max costume about letting me put on the costume and do his part of the show. Of course, I had not been trained, but I had foolish confidence that I could do it since I had seen the show so many times.

He let me.

I put on the costume, and, with a show in progress, found out I could not see at all through the mouth. I lurched onto the stage on all fours, missing the dog's mark, but I finally jumped onto Ariel and Eric for the closing scene and the curtain.

The moment the curtain closed, the cast member playing Ariel switched off her mike and said, "What the fuck is wrong with the dog?"

I reached up, took off the head, and said, "It's me. Dr. Rizzo."

She shook her head in disgust and walked away.

I had a very good relationship with that cast member. I had seen her in two off-property plays. I took her to see Kingdom Ariels. She once gifted me with an Easter basket. But I tarnished my reputation that day. Soon after this, she left for Hollywood, but I never saw her cast in anything after that.

Belle's Dress

The *Beauty and the Beast* stage show in The Theater of the Stars had a problem.

If you have never seen the show, you are missing a real treat. In fifteen minutes, the entire animated film is synopsized with every major song performed, the Beast transformation is performed before your very eyes, along with an amazing number of costume changes.

I wanted to see why I was treating so many of the Belles for knee injuries.

One afternoon after the last show, I went over to the theater with a show manager, a costumer, and a Beast. I asked them to walk me through the show from start to finish, including the costume changes.

Yes, I wore Belle's clothes.

We got through almost the entire show, and I could not discern how or why the Belles were getting injured.

Then, they put the gold ball gown on me. That dress weighed fifty pounds, or at least it did in those days.

When the Beast twirled me at the end of the dance, I stopped on the mark, but the inertia of the fifty-pound dress kept it going. My feet were planted, the dress kept turning, and my knees twisted very painfully.

I weigh considerably more than the 100-pound weight limit for the women who played Belle. I now knew exactly how these small, talented women were getting their knee ligaments strained.

I let the show manager know my findings. She told me Creative Costuming would never change that dress.

So the Creative Costuming mafia won over the health and safety of our cast. Again.

I say "again" because of Hunchback....

Fur Hunchback

When *The Hunchback of Notre Dame* was released, Creative Costuming came up with a Hunchback fur costume for character meet-and-greets at Studios.

Immediately, there was a major problem. The size and weight restrictions for the costume fit only the same cast members who were our mice. WDW does not go very far without Mickey and Minnie!

And all of our mice were injured.

Each of the injured cast, all small females, told me they had hurt themselves in the Quasi costume.

So I went out, got two character managers, and put on Quasi. The problem was immediately obvious.

Quasi was heavy. And, Quasi rested on the shoulders of the cast member using two non-padded metal shoulder hooks.

Wearing Quasi for only a few minutes contused my acromioclavicular joints, causing me pain for several weeks.

I explained what I had found to the managers who lifted the heavy thing off me. They told me Creative Costuming would never change the costume. The best they could do was wrap the shoulder hooks with padding instead of having bare metal on the shoulders of the petite, female cast members.

I urged Creative Costuming to add a waist belt to put the weight of the fiberglass costume on the hips instead of the shoulders. They refused.

The problem was solved when there were no mice in Studios because they had all been put on restrictions as a result of wearing Quasi. Without mice, Studios management made the executive decision to take Quasi out of meet-and-greets.

In all the years since, I have never seen Quasi reappear. I'm glad.

Toy Story Parade

The success of *Toy Story* inspired WDW to add a Toy Story Parade to Studios, a park that normally did not have a parade.

I was interested in the challenges of the parade, so I talked to parade management and asked to be put in a parade position for a day.

They chose for me the largest, heaviest thing they could find, clearly to make a point about the Creative Costuming mafia.

I was cast as the front end of Slinky Dog.

The day of my parade was a very hot, humid (read usual) summer day.

I was instructed to put on the undergarment, which was basically a top and bottom that looked suspiciously like long underwear designed for the arctic. A pair of calf-length socks went over my feet and legs

Then came thick, padded fur leggings.

I then donned a vest made of heavy canvas. This vest had multiple pockets, all of which contained ice. Similarly, a heavy canvas skull cap with ice pockets was placed on my head.

Next came Slinky Dog himself, a sixty-pound, top-heavy monstrosity that was suspended on military LBEs. I was familiar with LBEs, which stands for Load Bearing Equipment. Very heavy items are put on military members' backs by supporting a majority of the weight on the hips with a combination belt and shoulder rig.

I was then instructed to put on a headset with a live microphone, so a young lady in the back end of Slinky Dog could communicate instructions to me in the front.

Because of the design of Slinky's front end, the person in it cannot see. There is a tiny patch of foam disguising the viewing port, but it is more than eighteen inches from your face. The result is you can see through what amounts to a peephole only the things directly in front of you and at a significant distance. You have no side vision and have no idea what is closer than twenty feet immediately in front of you.

The back end of Slinky has a much better view, so she constantly gives directions to the front as to where to go. Hence the headset.

The route was about one mile through the studios, starting by Star Tours and ending next to Sid Cahuenga's One-of-a-Kind Shop.

Along the route, Slinky is supposed to bow to guests, turn left and right, and, "Remember, you must keep dancing! Never stop dancing!"

Controls for turning the head, blinking the eyes, and bowing are in both of your hands. The weight is on your hips and shoulders. It's hot. The back end of Slinky is talking non-stop. And you're dancing!

As soon as the parade stepped, I could see how incredibly difficult the job was for the regular cast. I may as well have closed my eyes since what I could see had nothing to do with the directions I was being given to walk—er, dance.

At one point, the back end urgently said, "Stop!! You're about to be hugged!"

An unseen little kid had broken free of an unseen parent then ran into the parade and grabbed my right leg. I never saw him or her, and I barely felt the kid through all of the padding I was wearing. I have to assume the parent got the kid because, after a few moments, Back End said, "Start dancing and go!"

By the end of the parade, every bit of ice in the skull cap and vest had melted. The cap and vest were soaked with hot water.

The crane—yes, it required a crane—came over and lifted Slinky off me after I was reminded to unlatch the LBE. Had I forgotten, I would have been lifted right off the ground by the crane.

I was a sweaty mess who took a shower and had to return to First Aid and see patients. First Aid is a clean, air conditioned building. The rest of the parade cast had to go into fur or do other outside, sweaty work.

The WDW cast is more remarkable than guests will ever realize.

Custodial and Guest Services—They Know Everything!

In my custodial whites.

Custodians At WDW Are Ubiquitous.

They are virtually everywhere, all of the time. Guests see custodians more than any other cast member.

For that reason, when cast members are first hired and go through Traditions Training, they are told that custodians have more guest interactions than any other cast members.

I certainly found that to be true when I did a custodial shift at Studios.

The head of Studios Custodial came over to First Aid to get me on the appointed day. We went to costuming and were issued our whites.

We then went into the park after the Toy Story parade had passed. There was a lot of litter to pick up.

But there was much more than litter to deal with.

I learned about the Code V kits inside the garbage can cases. When someone vomits, which is often at WDW, a Code V is called. Custodial, or any nearby cast member, can go to a garbage can housing, open the front, and find a bag of desiccant. Literally, I'm talking about human kitty litter.

After pouring the desiccant onto the vomit, and waiting for the magic to happen, custodians can then pan-and-broom the absorbed vomit and toss it into the trash.

Was it the case that, as a custodian, I had more guest interactions than any other cast member? Yes! I couldn't count the number of guests who approached me to ask questions. Where is the nearest restroom? What time is the parade? (It just ended). What time does the park close? What time does the park open? What time is the next Fantasmic? Will there be fireworks tonight? Where should I stand? What time is the next Hunchback show? The custodians had to know everything because, remember, WDW cast members are not permitted to say, "I don't know."

Guest Services People Are Truly Special

If you want to read about what it is like to work in Guest Services in WDW, I suggest two books: *Would You Like Magic with That?* and *The Ride Delegate*, both by Annie Salisbury and published by Theme Park Press. I've never met Annie, but I wish I had and would love to one day.

I did Guest Services at Studios one day as part of my ongoing effort to perform every job in the park in order to understand the mechanisms of injury and illness.

Dressed as a Plaid

My responsibilities were in two very different locations.

The first was in the Guest Services location, which is actually adjacent to First Aid. After getting into a plaid costume—there's a reason Guest Services cast members are called Plaids—I reported to the Guest Services manager. Of course, the manager knew better than to leave an untrained, inexperienced person such as myself alone at a Guest Services desk. She stood behind me and coached me as I heard one complaint after another from guests who were seeking something from WDW.

The range of complaints was legion. It's too hot here. It rains here. The lines are too long. The food costs too much. My ride broke down. My son vomited (never mentioning the vast amount of crap the kid ate before vomiting). The bus from the resort took too long. The air conditioning is too cold/hot/humid/dry.

Basically, guests spend a lot of money to go to WDW. Some of them try to get some or all of their money back by complaining to Guest Services.

If you are ever in the park, and you want to see a Guest Services person smile, go in to tell them you are only there to compliment a cast member. Cast member compliments, when they happen, are actually read to the cast in meetings and are put into the cast member's folder when it comes time for promotions or transfers.

My second job that day had to do with a celebrity.

An uncle from a popular sitcom was in the park. He was to get into a convertible and slowly be driven up Hollywood Boulevard from behind Sid's to the Chinese Theater. There, he was to get out of the car, make a few remarks to the guests from a podium, then put his hands in cement for the patio in front of the theater.

My job was to walk next to the uncle's car to assure no guests ran out from the sidewalk or threw something that could hit him.

When Uncle got to the Chinese Theater he exited the car and went to the podium. A Guest Services cast member then told him there was a very special Give Kids the World guest who wanted to meet the uncle. The uncle was told he was this kid's favorite person in the world.

Of course, the kid was brought to the podium. The uncle was most gracious. Until the uncle was not. The kid, who was intellectually challenged as well as suffering from a terminal illness, could not understand why he had to leave Uncle's side when it came time for Uncle to speak and put his hands in the cement. It was tense.

Finally, another Guest Services cast member gently and appropriately guided the child back to his parents. Uncle said a few forgettable words. A table was rolled out upon which sat a three-foot by three-foot wooden frame containing wet cement.

Uncle put his hands in the cement, scratched his name in the cement with a stick, wiped his hands with a cloth provided by another Guest Services cast member, then got back in the car.

Those of us assigned to the security detail then walked the car back down Hollywood Boulevard, backstage next to Sid's, and the job was done.

I asked the Guest Services manager what would happen to the cement that Uncle had personalized. I asked because there were a few such blocks in the Chinese Theater patio, but I had never seen any new ones emplaced. Many, many celebrities had the same sort of ceremony I had just participated in, but I never saw the cement blocks put in front of the Theater.

The manager told me Custodial waits for the cement to dry, then the cement is broken up with a sledge hammer and piled up backstage. She even showed me the pile.

Celebrity is fleeting....

6

The Giant Mouse

We were having a large number of cast members in Mice complain of eye irritation and upper respiratory problems. Some who did not have asthma were complaining of wheezing.

So, I went backstage and told a supervisor I needed to get into the Mickey costume.

This became *quite* the production. By the time I was in Mouse, there must have been thirty or forty cast members, all who normally wear fur, waiting to see me in the costume. All were telling me about the Mouse problems, although only a handful actually wore the costume. But fur people are a close-knit group.

Yes, I am *way* too tall for Mouse. So the pants were short. The shirt and jacket were too small. The shoes were ridiculous. But once I put on the head, I solved the mystery.

There was a distinct odor in the head. It didn't bother my eyes or upper airway, but I could definitely smell it.

Before I could take the costume off, however, about a million Disney rules were broken.

Photography backstage is *strictly prohibited.* But the manager was there and she wanted pictures.

Essentially, every fur character had his or her picture taken with the *Big Mickey*. People were dragging fur from everywhere. Characters that had not been seen on stage in forever were suddenly standing next to *Big Mickey* for a picture. Then the cast, out of costume, had their pictures taken with *Big Mickey*. I have no idea what happened to those pictures. I sure wish I had a few!

It turns out the heads were being sprayed between sets with a new chemical cleaner. The cleaner was irritating to some of the cast.

It was a simple fix that should not have taken a Disney Doc to get into the costume to figure out. But I'm glad it did! That was one experience I will never forget.

Tower of Terror

As part of my ongoing effort to learn about all of the jobs at Studios, I arranged to spend part of a day with the manager of the Twilight Zone Tower of Terror.

What an astounding attraction.

At a cost of $140,000,000—yup, 140 million dollars—the Twilight Zone Tower of Terror was a major addition to Studios.

The manager took me everywhere in the attraction. The elevator motor in the top of the building has a cable that attaches to the top of the car, of course. But the motor also has a cable that runs down the entire height of the building, through pulleys, and attaches to the bottom of the cars, as well.

So, when the cars are descending, they are pulled down by the huge motors at the top of the shaft, so that the drop accelerates faster than gravity!

The attraction actually has two shafts. Upon reaching the top of the first elevator shaft, the cars leave that shaft and follow an electronic path into the second shaft—the second shaft with the cable above and below the cars.

The manager and I stood in an alcove next to where the cars leave the first shaft.

The guests rode by no more than two feet from us but couldn't see us as that alcove was designed for an observer should one be needed. After the car passed, we walked behind it and watched it latch itself into the second, more thrilling shaft. Passengers could have turned around and seen us walking behind the car, but the manager assured me *no one* has ever done that—there's just too much to see straight ahead!

The photo that is taken in the second, thrilling shaft is one guests really should purchase. Sadly, some guests never get to see their photos. There is a room in the Tower of Terror filled with monitors for watching the guests during every moment of the attraction for their safety. Some guests are idiots and ruin the pictures for the rest of the people in their car by flashing their breasts, displaying middle fingers, even—and I don't know how they manage it—mooning at the time of the photo.

When that happens, if the photo monitors cannot photoshop the offenders from the picture, the picture simply disappears, meaning that the rest of the guests in that car cannot get their photo.

That is a shame, as there are *many, many* guests who are making their one and only Disney visit. Losing a photo memory because another guest is an idiot is very sad.

8

The Great Movie Ride

Hosting The Great Movie Ride

Continuing my effort to learn every job in Studios, I approached the manager of The Great Movie Ride and asked to learn to spiel the attraction. I had seen a few cowboys as patients and wanted to discover their mechanism of injury.

The manager arranged a day and time to train two days hence. She then handed me a forty-six-page script and told me not to bother coming back if I hadn't learned all of it.

Fortunately for me, I had ridden The Great Movie Ride many, many times. But I was surprised at the complexity of the script. For each scene, the spieling host had multiple options as to what to say. I was required to learn all of them.

The first thing the manager had me do was walk the ride with her. We did this during a full show with passengers in the ride vehicle! The manager told me guests never, ever turn around to see what is behind them, so that spieling hosts are evaluated simply by having a supervisor walk the ride behind the vehicle.

Then, in full costume, the manager had me spiel a ride from start to finish in a vehicle devoid of guests. There was a full ride vehicle in front and behind, so I had to get the timing right.

I was doing the B ride, which was the ride with the cowboys. The A ride, with the gangsters, did not have the spieling host do the Anubis scene.

So, when I got to the shootout, I had to leave the vehicle and interact with the animatronics on stage. Then, I had to exit through a door just before the explosion (with real, hot fire), run up a staircase and cross over the track in a narrow walkway, put on the Anubis Robes, and get back on stage to do the scene with the scarab. This was followed by rapidly going down a very steep set of steps that were poorly lit, returning to the vehicle, and resuming the ride.

Should the hosts have been wearing hearing protection? Yes, the guns fire real blanks and are loud. Did it make sense that I had treated hosts who had fallen down the Anubis steps? You bet. The steps were steep and *very* dark and the action had to be performed quickly.

The manager told me I had done well enough that she wondered if I wanted to pick up some extra shifts!

Is it true that some cast members have had sex in the hollow front of the elephant in the Tarzan scene? I cannot personally attest to that, but I can see how the location would lend itself to such activities.

Disney Transportation

I spent time with two forms of Disney transportation. One was boring, and one was quite the opposite.

The monorail was simply boring. I rode with a cast member who piloted the monorail on the resort loop. It was a simple matter of stopping, starting, and trying not to hit the monorail in front of you. The repetition was deadly. I was amazed that the monorail pilots could tolerate such a repetitive job.

That said, the potential for problems on the monorail is very real. A breakdown would necessitate evacuation using Reedy Creek Fire and Rescue. There are places on the resort loop that are over water, where evacuation would be nearly impossible.

The monorail pilot has no access to the cars behind her, so if a guest uses the emergency intercom to report a problem in a car, the best a pilot can do is continue to the next resort for help.

The evening and night I spent with a bus driver was quite different from the monorail experience. The bus I rode was doing a loop between Pleasure Island, the Beach Club Resort, and the Yacht Club Resort.

Yes, driving around and around the same path was boring, but much less so than the monorail. Pleasure Island was Disney's attempt to compete with the nightlife of Church Street in Orlando and City Walk at Universal. Alcohol was served in abundance. So, as the night progressed, the drivers sharing the road with my bus were more and more intoxicated. My driver told me that near misses were a matter of routine, especially as the night wore on.

Inebriated guests vomiting on the bus was a common occurrence. It was up to the driver to clean up the mess.

Guests either being rowdy or passing out was also a normal occurrance. The driver had a calm demeanor, but it was clear he would brook no nonsense from the drunken guests who got on his bus.

At a bus stop at Pleasure Island, there was a young man who passed out, lying on the bench with an arm over the wooden back. I asked the driver what we should do for him. He said, "Nothing. He will eventually wake up or Security will get him."

What bothered me as a physician was that this guest stayed on that bench with his arm draped over the hard back for the entire time I was on the bus, which was about three hours. The chance for him to have developed damage to the major nerve in his arm and hand was significant.

The driver told me that unconscious guests were a nightly occurrence and the policy was to simply let them lie where they were. I hoped this guy did not develop a palsy as a result of his drinking binge that night.

10

Studios

Alice Is My Hero

When Studios opened, one of the face characters in the park was Alice. The same Alice found in *Wonderland.* First Aid in Studios at that time was not well designed for seeing cast members.

Guests walked in one door, and directly opposite the guest entrance, across from the nurse's desk, was the cast entrance. So, cast members had to be careful to enter or exit only when no guests were coming, going, or waiting in the guest waiting area.

To make matters worse, the only place cast members could wait to be seen was a bench on the opposite side of the nurse's island from the guest area.

One morning, Alice came in and sat on the cast bench, waiting to be seen. Her head was visible above the nurse's island if a guest should walk in, which is exactly what happened.

In full costume, the moment a guest opened the door, Alice threw herself onto the floor so the guest could not see her from across the nurse's island.

I waited for the guest to go into a room with a nurse, then went to get Alice and brought her to a cast exam room.

Alice had a fever of 103.6 degrees and was suffering from strep throat confirmed by a rapid strep test. She was feeling miserable, but despite how bad she felt, she threw herself on the floor rather than break character and destroy the magic for a guest.

This kid was my hero that day.

Sad Server

One early afternoon the nurses took a call from the 50's Prime Time Café which was almost directly behind First Aid. The manager said one of his servers was unconscious in the cast ladies room and asked if I would come.

Of course I hurried over, wondering why the manager had called us instead of a Reedy Creek alpha unit (Disney's code for an ambulance).

In the ladies room, I found a server in full costume, slumped on a commode in a stall. When I approached her, she slid onto the floor. She reeked of alcohol.

Sadly, this nineteen-year-old was passed-out drunk just after noon while at work.

Alcoholism is a terrible disease. I hope her losing her job that day was the rock-bottom alcoholics frequently have to hit before they find the wherewithal to seek help.

Hunchback

While I was a cast member, Disney released *The Hunchback of Notre Dame*. This movie was a big hit that spawned a stage show adaptation at the Studios.

That show spawned several unforgettable memories.

The Hunchback, himself, wore an *extremely* heavy costume. Because of the height and weight restrictions of the costume, the cast members playing the Hunchback were small men. The costume, with all of its many layers and the hunch, weighed close to thirty pounds.

During the performance, besides running around the stage, the Hunchback had to run up and down steps, climb up and down ladders, and swing on a rope from one side of the stage to the other.

The stage and theater were outdoors located where now there is part of Star Wars Galaxy's Edge.

So, the cast member playing Hunchback was sweating—*profusely*—during the performance.

Having watched this show from preproduction rehearsals though multiple performances, I was concerned about how much fluid the Hunchback was losing through sweat in performing multiple summer shows.

I went backstage one summer afternoon and asked the Hunchback to separately weigh himself and his costume at the beginning of a shift.

That day, after his first show—an afternoon performance—I asked him to take his entire costume off and weighed it again. The costume was wringing wet with his sweat, and it was three-and-one-half pounds heavier after the show than it had been at the beginning. As water weighs 8.34 pounds/gallon, the Hunchback had sweated over four tenths of a gallon, or approximately 1 2/3 quarts of sweat in a single performance!

It was no surprise that the Hunchbacks did not feel well at the end of their shifts.

I was concerned that a dehydrated Hunchback might become seriously injured climbing up and down ladders and swinging on a rope. I was also not surprised when the Hunchback cast members said they never urinated during an entire shift, despite drinking water after shows.

Once I knew how much the cast member I had measured was losing in sweat, I discussed fluid replacement with not only the cast but with show management. I instructed how much water a Hunchback needed to drink to avoid acute dehydration injuries and possible kidney stones.

I was told that was too much water, as the cast members did not want to go to the trouble of removing the lower part of the costume to urinate between shows.

You can lead a horse to water….

Esmerelda

I do not know how many times I saw one particular Esmeralda. This was a young lady who definitely looked the part and had a beautiful singing voice.

She repeatedly came to First Aid for groin pulls.

Part of the show had Esmeralda singing, dancing, and ending a dance in a split. This Esmeralda would strain her inguinal ligament doing the split.

Foolishly, I assumed that the cast members playing Esmeralda were trained dancers. I was disabused of that notion when this cast member told me she was "a singer who moves well." That is an actual category for hiring cast members.

So, this Esmeralda was not used to doing a split, much less after a vigorous dance, and even less after doing multiple performances per day.

I told her the only way she would allow her strained inguinal ligament to heal was with rest.

Of course, she told me that was impossible. She stated if she took off even one show, she would be replaced.

I have no idea if that was true, but she certainly believed it. She kept doing the show, continued to hurt herself, and continued to see me for groin pain for which I could only give ibuprofen as she refused to rest.

Laverne

Laverne was a gargoyle who sang in a creaky, gravely voice. One of the cast playing Laverne was a woman I had known as Belle in the Beauty and the Beast stage show at Studios.

This woman had a truly lovely singing voice. She played Belle so professionally and convincingly that the guests really believed they had seen Belle come to life before their eyes.

But after about a year as Belle, Disney decided this cast member was now too old to play the part, and re-cast her as a gargoyle.

The woman's precious vocal cords were insulted at each show as she sang and spoke in that gravely voice.

To make the show more challenging for her, she was also cast as a villager who sang the line, "I ask for love, I can possess" during the God Help the Outcasts number. She had to make a quick change from Laverne to the villager, sing her line in her beautiful voice, then quickly change back to Laverne and strain her vocal cords for each show.

In 2019, I saw this same woman playing Befana, the Italian Christmas Witch, during the Epcot Holiday Festival. They surely found a way to ugly her up.

The Juggler

The Hunchback preshow involved a juggler who was a show in himself. Excellent at his job, part of his preshow included bringing a child from the audience onto the stage and interacting with the kid.

As I had taken care of him several times for both illness and injury, we knew each other well enough that I could ask a favor from time to time.

Whenever my family visited the Studios, I would go backstage and ask the Juggler to pick one of my daughters for his act. He always obliged. My girls, who were young, always thought that being picked from the audience was a standard part of the show!

Likewise, Quasimodo would tear a large playing card at the end of the show—a heart—and give it to a child saying, "You have my heart." My girls have theirs framed and autographed by Quasimodo.

Pocahontas

After Hunchback closed, the same theater was used for a live adaptation of *Pocahontas*. There were so many ankle and knee injuries from that show that there were times it could not be performed.

For *Pocahontas*, the stage was raked. That means the stage, instead of being level, was at an angle toward the audience. Running around, jumping, and dancing on a raked stage is a prescription for orthopedic injuries.

That show, short-lived as it was, was nothing but trouble. From a Health Services perspective, knee and ankle injuries were simply expected.

From a management perspective, the cast was very demanding. When the show closed, the cast lodged a major protest against the sycamore tree, part of the set, being taken down. You might remember the line, "How high does the sycamore grow? If you cut it down, you'll never know." Well, the cast did not want the set's sycamore taken down.

That show was *difficult*.

A Stupid Question

Included in the Toy Story Parade were very large floats. Of course, these floats were quite heavy and ran on large, wide wheels.

Incredibly, a Disney executive once asked me what would happen if a float ran over a child.

Although the answer seemed patently obvious, I had to give this person a quantifiable answer without actually finding some kid and running her over to see what would happen.

So, one afternoon, I got a float driver and the curious executive and walked over to the Brown Derby restaurant. Entering the kitchen, I asked the executive chef to please give me a steak that had a bone, such as a T-bone.

The chef gave me an absolutely beautiful steak that Disney would have charged at least thirty dollars for.

We walked out to where the floats were backstage. I put the steak on the ground in front of a float wheel and asked the driver to run over it.

The result was a T-bone pancake that we had to scrape from the hot asphalt.

I considered that a stupid question answered in a stupid way.

Muppet*Vision 3D

I really loved the Muppet*Vision 3D attraction. It was a virtual masterpiece.

One of the characters is Sweetums, who appears in person during the show.

In my ongoing effort to do every possible job in Studios, one afternoon I went to the Muppet Theater and entered through the cast door. There I found two young men who were the cast members alternating playing Sweetums. I talked to them about what it was like to be in the costume and if there were any problems with it.

Then I asked to try it on.

They were more than happy to oblige.

The problem, of course, was that the shows are continuous with 564 guests seeing a show every fifteen minutes.

The only way I was going to try on the costume was if I could do a show.

I assured the cast members I knew the show, having seen it so many times. They looked at each other and, fooled into complacency by my shirt and tie, put me in and wound me up to do a show.

I did the show—sort of. By that, I mean I am certain I was not ever on the correct mark. My entrance was slightly late and my exit was very late. I never, never saw where I was going. I could only vaguely see some blurry light and basically felt my way in front of the penguin orchestra.

When I got off stage, the two cast members could not get the costume off me fast enough. I think they had figured out their show management was not involved with my being there and asking questions, and I had done what had to be considered a poor show.

In every show on property, show management regularly sits in the audience to assure quality. These guys realized that my bad show would be on them if a manager was in the audience.

I never found out if there was a problem for those two trusting souls. But I did find out how difficult it was to play Sweetums.

Indiana Jones Epic Stunt Spectacular

This show fascinated me for several reasons. Because it was a stunt show, I was surprised that I never saw any injuries arising from performances or rehearsals. Plus, I was engrossed by the logistics of moving multi-ton set pieces, interacting with an airplane with spinning propellers, and avoiding fire, explosions, and gunfire.

I spent some time talking with the show manager, and he agreed to let me do every stunt in the show except the high fall.

To be clear, I did not do any of the stunts in an actual show except to push the boulder up the incline. The rest were done when the show was dark.

First, the boulder. It is a giant, hollow, inflated rubber ball. Yes, it's heavy, but nothing like it appears. If Indy were ever actually to be run over by it, he would be just fine.

Then, the other stunts:

In shirt and tie, I was taken through the entire show, doing every stunt including the slide for life. These were so safe and simple I believe anyone motivated to do so could perform them. The stunt actors were just that: actors. They made the stunts look challenging and dangerous, when they were not at all.

The best part was the gunfire. The machine guns were all "weapons" that fired propane gas, making a small flame when the triggers were pulled. The actual sound of the "weapons" was a quiet "pffft" each time a flame was produced. All of the sounds of gunfire were sound effects.

One Sunday afternoon, with the show manager's permission, I took my young kids backstage to see Dad do stunts. The stunt actors really got into it and made me look like a hero. They placed my two daughters, quite small at the time, in the cockpit of the airplane and allowed them to "fire" the machine gun. They laughed so hard when the gun went, "pffft, pffft, pfft!"

One day, one of the other Disney Docs, one known for never having gone into the parks or having anything to do with learning the cast jobs, asked me what the Indy show was like. I took him over and demonstrated the stunts for him. The show manager offered him the slide for life. He shook his head and walked away. He was a weenie.

Sorcery in the Sky Fireworks

What a show! *Sorcery in the Sky* was fantastic. I loved it and wanted to know how it was done.

There were two aspects to the show from my perspective: show control and the mechanics of the show itself.

I spent an evening with the show's control manager in the control booth that is upstairs from the ABC Theater, which now hosts the Frozen Singalong. Amazingly, the show controller has no windows through which to see the show. He or she controls it entirely from a panel below video screens. His computer coordinates the lights, lasers, music, and fireworks. He really oversees the computer!

The mechanics were a different story. Going with the armorers to set the firework charges, which was done in the afternoon, I learned how seriously these people took their work. Their work was sincerely hazardous, yet I never once saw an armorer as a patient. They were careful and deliberate, always.

The highlight of my learning about the show happened the night I spent on the roof of the Chinese Theater with the onstage show manager. She and I climbed the stairs on the outside back of the theater and hid below the roof lip so no guests could see us.

Fireworks went off all around us! Sparks and debris rained down on us! Then, on cue from the control manager's computer, Sorcerer Mickey's giant internal fan started up and Mickey inflated, towering over the roof as I crouched at the hem of his robe. At just the right moment, firework sparks flew from Mickey's outstretched finger.

It was loud, exciting, and a once-in-a-lifetime experience!

Wait, one question. Where did all of the firework debris land? At the time, the debris landed on the cast parking lot behind the Studios. Cast members knew if they parked there in the evening there was a good chance debris would hit, and possibly damage, their cars. The Company made it clear there would be no compensation for damaged cars—parking was at the cast member's risk.

Now, of course, what used to be cast parking is part of the park encompassing Toy Story Land and Galaxy's Edge. Fireworks are now set off northwest of the park.

12

EPCOT

Getting an Earful

What patients told me about their injuries and what really happened were *often* entirely different. (By the way, this was and is true of all patients, not just cast members.)

EPCOT First Aid is behind the Baby Care Center near the Odyssey. At the time I worked there, cast members entered a back door directly across from the Mexico Pavilion.

One day, a gaggle of international cast members from Mexico accompanied a young Mexican woman who had a torn, freely bleeding earlobe. Her story was that she was changing her costume, caught something on her earring, and tore her earlobe from the piercing downward.

This story did not seem to fit the injury in front of me, which was a severely torn earlobe that, indeed, included the piercing where an earring had been. It was likely that she had gotten into a fight with one of her colleagues who grabbed the earring and violently tore it through the lobe.

I spent a considerable amount of time with this cast member cleaning the lobe and stopping the bleeding. Any of the other Disney Docs would have sent her to the hospital, but, as a surgeon, this was something I could take care of.

I did a plastics-type closure to minimize the scarring. I made it abundantly clear that, if she wanted the scarring to be minimized, I needed to see her to remove the sutures. I scheduled a follow-up appointment.

I probably saved the company several thousands of dollars by being able to handle the injury in-house.

On the appointed day and time, I awaited the cast member, who never showed up. I checked with the other Disney Docs across property, as well as the computer, to see if she had returned to one of them at an incorrect time. She had not.

I then walked across the alley to the Mexico Pavilion, entered through a side door, and sought out a coordinator. No one had seen this cast member, and no one seemed to want to talk to me.

In fact, she was never seen again.

I could only assume that the alleged fight causing the injury was enough to have her sent back to Mexico.

I hope she found someone there to remove the sutures in a timely manner.

Executive Meetings Were Surprising

As a full-time cast member who was considered an executive, from time to time, I had to represent Health Services at various executive meetings.

I was actually looking forward to one that was called to discuss the new EPCOT fireworks extravaganza.

At the extreme southwest corner of Property, off Route 192, there are some offices housing a wide range of Disney services. Many executive-type meetings used to be held there.

So, at the appointed day and time, I left EPCOT First Aid and drove down for my first meeting in these previously unknown-to-me buildings.

There were two meetings on my agenda that day.

The first was with the creative folks. These idea-people were and are—there is no other word for it—*Amazing*.

They presented a concept for an EPCOT fireworks show that would be, as they described it, an *extravaganza*!

The part I remember most clearly, including a vivid memory of the large artist's renderings they used, were to be the dancing cranes.

The idea was that multi-articulated metal cranes would sit all day, unseen, under the water of the World Showcase Lagoon. During the show, these cranes would arise from the water, and, because they were multi-articulated, would dance to the music accompanying the show. The cranes would also shoot lasers and fireworks. It was an astounding idea and an impressive presentation.

I remember thinking, as I listened and looked at the renderings, that there could be some issues with submerging metal, joints, hydraulics, electrical connections, lasers, and fireworks canisters. But, who was I to ask? There was no reason for a Disney Doc to be in this meeting, except that it was routine to invite us.

This was my first such meeting, and I believed what I had heard was the plan for the next EPCOT fireworks show. I assumed the electromechanical bugs had been worked out.

The follow-up meeting, held five minutes after the creative folks left, was with the engineers.

The topic was the same upcoming fireworks show.

The engineers did not have dazzling renderings. In fact, the engineers' presentation was entirely verbal.

The engineers made it clear that dancing cranes, the very heart of the creative folks' presentation, were *never* going to happen.

They went into great detail as to how those cranes would never, ever work. They explained how submerging something that had to be able to emerge and dance, especially in the water of World Showcase Lagoon, was ridiculous.

They reminded the executives that fireworks debris had been put into the lagoons since EPCOT's first day, and, consequently, the water was corrosive. The cranes would be submerged in corrosive water, adding to the normal issues involved when water mixes with electrics and hydraulics.

The engineers talked about the incredible amount of power that would have to be routed underwater; the water's corrosive action of the cranes' joints; the impossibility of maintaining lasers while under water; and the impossibility of loading gunpowder-filled fireworks and assuring they would actually work after emerging from the water. The engineers went on and on about how they would never sign off on the dancing cranes.

I learned a lesson that day: creative presentations do not always reflect reality. WDW spent, and still spends, a *lot* of money on ideas and idea people. Quite a bit of the work of these creative people never sees the light of day.

A Deep-Sixed Lawsuit

When I was assigned to two weeks of training to be a Disney executive, one of the presenters was a Disney attorney. He told this story, and I have no reason to doubt him.

Where now is found The Seas with Nemo and Friends used to be Sea Base Alpha. The queue to the Sea Base Alpha dark ride told the story of a base far under the ocean. The actual dark ride took guests to Sea Base Alpha on the bottom of the ocean. The guests then could explore the EPCOT Living Seas until they decided to return to EPCOT Center.

The exit from Living Seas appeared to be a bank of elevators. Guests entered an elevator, and after the doors closed the elevator vibrated while lights in the corners of the car presented the illusion of a rapid ascent from the ocean floor to the land.

Moments later, doors on the opposite side of the elevator from which the guests entered opened and the guests were back in EPCOT.

Needless to say, guests did not *really* go to the middle of the ocean on the dark ride. Guests were not *really* on the bottom of the ocean while investigating the Living Seas. Guests did not *really* ascend from the bottom of the middle of the ocean in an elevator that somehow got them back to WDW. In fact, the elevator did not actually move at all. A door opened on one side, the car vibrated and lights flashed, then the door on the other side of the car opened.

There were exit doors on either side of the bank of elevators that one could simply open and walk through, leaving the Living Seas to continue the visit to EPCOT.

A guest brought suit against WDW because she claimed the elevator taking her from the ocean floor back to EPCOT ascended too quickly and her ears popped, causing her great distress.

It was the policy of WDW, when I was there, to never settle a suit out of court. WDW gets sued multiple times every single day.

The majority of the suits are frivolous and are just guests seeing a deep pocket and wanting something for nothing. But WDW defended every suit. This one is a perfect example as to why.

Tapestry of Nations Parade

EPCOT put on the Tapestry of Nations parade from 1999 until 2001. It was a strange parade with huge puppets, people on stilts, and lots and lots of huge flags.

It is possible the parade designers failed to notice that Florida has a rainy season and a hurricane season.

The wind blows a lot in Florida. It is hot, so people tend to forget the wind until they are on tall stilts, trying to work huge puppets, or trying to manage gigantic flags.

Since the parade went around the World Showcase Lagoon, the route was 1.2 miles long.

It should be obvious there were a *lot* of injuries to the cast as a result of this parade.

One afternoon, I found the parade manager and asked to operate as many of the parade items as possible. He would not allow me on stilts, thus I was unable to try to work a puppet.

He gave me a flag, which was about twenty feet tall, and I tried to walk backstage with it in what was a mild wind.

Managing that flag was murder. Even in a slight breeze, it tried to pull me over. It was clear why I was seeing the injuries I was seeing.

I tried to discuss the danger of the parade with park management. They were not interested in hearing what I had to say. The show was the show, and the cast was expected to put on that show regardless of injuries.

In 2001, the parade was modified to become the Tapestry of Dreams. Injuries to both cast and guests continued. Finally the parade was discontinued in March of 2003.

Thank goodness!

Living with the Land

EPCOT's Land Pavilion has a relaxing boat ride attraction called Living with the Land. The boat goes through a story about ecology, including passing through areas where actual food is being grown.

The recorded spiel for Living with the Land states that the food is served in restaurants throughout WDW. It implies that The Land Pavilion is a major supplier of WDW's food.

New cast members going through Traditions training are also told that food from The Land Pavilion is sourced to restaurants throughout WDW.

Once, I was speaking with a new Cinderella/Belle who said she had been told that *all* of the food in the WDW restaurants came from The Land Pavilion.

There are a few plants in the pavilion. There are a few farmed fish. A handful of vegetables and fruits, and a few fish may be harvested from time to time. But it is just part of the Disney magic—part of the show—to tell cast members and guests that The Land Pavilion is a major supplier of food for the parks.

At best, there might be a few salads in one of the restaurants from time to time, but I am not even sure about that. Never had I seen any plants or fish actually harvested, and I never found a single cast member who told me their job involved harvesting, cleaning, and distributing food to the restaurants.

On the contrary, I spent time with the people delivering food to the restaurants. The food came in big trucks, purchased using massive contracts from suppliers off property.

The volume of food served at WDW is almost beyond imagination. I spent one day with a restaurant manager in Studios. He showed me how hamburgers were produced by a machine backstage in one of the smallest, least busy venues at Studios. He told me the venue served one thousand beef patties per hour. Each of those burgers needed lettuce, tomato, condiments, and a bun. To assume those foodstuffs came from the tiny plot of soil seen in The Land Pavilion was laughable.

The American Adventure

What a wonderful show! *The American Adventure* is mysterious to those who are paying attention, as it seems impossible for the acts in this show to appear and disappear as they do. Large set pieces with audioanimatronic characters appear from below the stage or from the wings, seemingly defying the laws of physics. Seriously, how can so many large, moving objects occupy the same space at the same time?

The answer is that they don't.

I spent a few hours with the head of *The American Adventure* maintenance. He told me there had actually been a death in the past in the area he was taking me to. I cannot independently confirm that, but, having seen how *The American Adventure* works, I can believe it.

Below the stage, and running behind it, all of the many sets are on conveyors and turntables. When the show starts, no human had better be in the spaces below or backstage! The set pieces move on and off elevators that lift them for guest viewing, then move away to allow another piece to move in. It is mechanical choreography like nothing I have ever seen.

A person in the wrong place during the show certainly could be crushed to death.

The area is securely closed to people during shows. Not just red lines but red obstructions keep anyone who absolutely has to be below stage during a show in a safe location. Watching the movements from one of those locations was mesmerizing.

While that is something very few are privileged to see, suffice it to say *The American Adventure* is not only awe-inspiring for the story it tells, but for the Disney magic that makes it happen.

Magic Kingdom

I Want To Be a Princess

One extremely busy afternoon, I was seeing one injury or illness after another in Magic Kingdom First Aid. There were so many cast-member patients that the hall was filled to standing-room-only.

I went into a room where I found a young lady sitting on the exam table. When I asked her what I could do for her, she whipped off her top and bra quickly and said, "Do you think my breasts are too small?"

This was not what I expected.

I excused myself and got a nurse to chaperone the visit.

When we returned to the room, this young lady sat, topless, and repeated her question.

The nurse was great. She produced a gown from a drawer and covered the patient, saying, "Honey, you need to put this on."

Through tears, the patient explained why she had come.

The bottom line was that this cast member had repeatedly auditioned to be a face character, specifically a princess. She had just come from another audition where she had, again, been rejected.

The people who chose the face characters used specific criteria. Height, weight, and facial characteristics are the priorities, so that the cast members can be made to look as much like a cartoon princess as possible once the wigs, makeup, and costumes are added.

This young lady didn't have the facial bone structure the company was looking for.

But, she was sure it was because her breasts were not big enough. Through sobs, she said she was planning to get a boob job so she could be a princess.

I tried to tell her that breast size was *not* one of the selection criteria for any of the princess face characters, but it was clear she did not believe me.

This young woman was an attractive person whose body was in perfect proportion for her height and weight. Making herself into a Barbie Doll would actually make her less likely to be selected for a face character.

I never saw her again and still wonder if she went to the expense and pain of breast implants for what was a goal her facial bone structure would not allow.

Dancing Is *Not* for the Weak Ankled

I have two intelligent, talented, and beautiful daughters. Both grew up to be teachers, and I could not be more proud of them. Both of them danced from the time they were two years old. For a few years, they danced at a studio in Kissimmee that prided itself on "putting more dancers into Disney than any other studio." Of course, that may have been because of the location, near WDW and populated by students who were locals.

Being a Disney dancer is a *hard* job. I saw many, many dancers who damaged their ankles while dancing in Kingdom's 3:00 parade.

The 3:00 parade started at Splash Mountain, went through Frontier Land, through Liberty Square, around the Hub, then down Main Street, U.S.A. to exit on-stage at the Firehouse. Main Street, U.S.A. has real streetcar tracks.

The streetcars were once an attraction guests could ride. In Disneyland, the streetcars were an "A" ticket. Now at WDW, the streetcars are primarily used to bring fur characters up and down Main Street, U.S.A. for guests to photograph.

So, the streetcar tracks were deep, genuine, and used every day.

If you have ever tried to push a stroller up Mainstreet, U.S.A. you know about those tracks. Stroller wheels are drawn to the tracks as if magnetized. Heaven knows how many strollers have tipped their little passengers out when Mom or Dad, in a hurry, has caught a front wheel in the track.

Wheelchairs are also *quite* prone to catch in the tracks. Guest after guest has come to a screeching stop, sometimes tipping over, when their wheelchair wheel got caught in the tracks.

So, of course, with great regularity WDW's dancers found their feet in the tracks.

WDW dancers are professionals. They know better than to look at their feet when dancing the parade. When the dancers got to Main Street, U.S.A., legions of them would plant a foot in the track, turn, and damage an ankle or knee.

What is amazing is how often the injured dancer would keep smiling and dancing until the end of parade, only to have to be carried into First Aid.

Disney had a cheesy solution for a while. Prior to the parade, a cast member was assigned to put long pieces of plastic into the tracks to level the track's depression with the rest of the street. These pieces of plastic were called cheese. After the parade, the cast member, pulling a large dolly, would pick up the cheese so the streetcars could run again.

The cheese helped the dancers to some degree, but created its own problems. The street is asphalt, the track is steel, and the cheese is plastic. When trying to make a dance turn, the dancer's foot would have different coefficients of friction on the sole as part of the sole would simultaneously be on all three kinds of surface, leading to slips and more ankle and knee damage.

None of the dancers' challenges were ameliorated by the heat or by the fact that the dancers wore *heavy* costumes.

These dancers made little more than minimum wage and could not afford to be put off work. They would beg to somehow magically be healed of their injuries, but frequently needed splints, casts, or even surgery.

Fur

Costumed characters are divided into FUR and FACE. Fur characters are anyone who wears a mask as part of the costume.

There was a 100 per cent injury rate in fur characters during my time as a Disney Doc.

Often the injury was from the costume itself. The heads of the costumes have gone through multiple evolutions, some of them *heavy*. The heads are out of proportion to reality, many times larger than the bodies they perch upon.

Of course, there is a height and weight restriction for a cast member in a fur costume. For mice, ducks, and hunchbacks, they were once expected to be no taller than four feet and weighing less than 100 pounds.

Putting a large, out-of-proportion head on one of those little females, placing them on stage, and having them animate the character was a major challenge to their necks. Remember, fur characters cannot speak. These characters communicate with exaggerated head movements. That large, heavy head had a lot of inertia when it got moving while nodding or turning, pulling on the cast members' tiny necks.

Neck, back, and shoulder injuries were a matter of course for the cast.

Then there were the guests. There was a special category of guest that would spend good money to get a ticket with the sole intent of attacking fur characters. These guests were invariably some large teenage males who thought putting Mickey in a headlock was hilarious.

The little girl in the costume had no defense.

Having no peripheral vision, she would look straight ahead through a tiny port disguised with foam. She could barely see at all, and only straight ahead into the distance. She could not see down or to the sides. So, when a guest stood next to her for a photo, she had no warning if he suddenly put her in a headlock, bending her over and causing the heavy head to pull in the direction of gravity while enclosing her neck in the crook of his elbow and pulling up.

The escorts could never stop this kind of behavior. Escorts had to be out of the photos, so they were far enough away that they never had time to intervene. The guests who came to the park just to hurt fur characters invariably ran away as soon as they performed their deed, so security rarely, if ever, caught them.

One weekend at Studios, a national cheerleading championship was being held. Cheerleading teams from all over the country came to compete, and the football teams came with them to cheer the cheerleaders.

So many football players hilariously put the fur characters in headlocks that every single cast member who fit in Mickey, Minnie, Donald, Daisy, and Hunchback costumes had to be taken off duty. Several were sent to the hospital, and all required physical therapy. For over a week, there were no mice in Studios because of this boorish, criminal guest behavior.

Such rude behavior from paying guests always astounded me. I wonder if it would have made any difference if they had known that the fur characters were really young, petite females who sweated through their thirty minutes on stage and thirty minutes off stage for an entire shift while animating those heavy costumes.

Face characters had their own set of problems. While injuries were uncommon, there was no shortage of gropes and costume grabs for the women in face character.

Face characters were primarily princesses. The correct way for an adult male to have his picture taken with a princess is to put his hand on his hip, with the crook of his elbow out so the princess can put her arm through his. Face characters are trained to guide the average adult male guest into this pose.

But there are those adult males who insist on grabbing the princess around the waist and pulling her *hard* against him. Or groping her breast. Or trying to pull her costume down to expose her breast. Or grabbing her buttock.

Some guests think this kind of behavior is hilarious. It's not.

Lice

This episode is a combination Kingdom and Studios event.

I had made friends with Ariel from Voyage of the Little Mermaid, a woman with a beautiful singing voice who was a truly great actress in off-property productions.

One day when working at Kingdom, I had to go to Studios for something. I saw Ariel, and we got to talking. She told me she had never seen Ariel at Kingdom.

The 20,000 Leagues Under the Sea: Submarine Voyage had been filled in, and in its place were a themed splash play area and an Ariel meet-and-greet.

The queue for Ariel would go through a rocky grotto until, after many twists and turns, there sat Ariel. Children could sit next to Ariel on her rock and have their picture taken while spending a few seconds speaking with the mermaid.

There was a backstage area from which you could watch the interactions without being seen. This backstage area was connected by an outdoor catwalk to the Ariel dressing room, which had many, many wigs—different sizes for the different head sizes of the cast members playing Ariel.

The catwalk was an attraction in itself. It ran along the top of a wall that was a sheer drop to the back entrance of the tunnels upon which Kingdom is built. Standing on the catwalk and looking in one direction you could see the spires of the castle. Turn around and you were looking straight down several stories to the top of trash, buses, and cast members coming and going into and out of the tunnel.

I took Studios Ariel onto the catwalk and to the backstage viewing area. She was impressed, but I'm not really sure in what way. She sang and acted in the show, experienced the special effect of converting from fin to legs, and was, in her way, a star. But she never interacted with guests. She never gave an autograph. Whenever she walked through Kingdom, no one recognized her. I think she missed having guest interaction.

But she absolutely did not envy what I told her when I took her to the Kingdom Ariel's dressing room. As she looked at the long row of wigs on Styrofoam heads, I told her we had recently had an outbreak of lice that infected every one of the wigs. We had had to close Ariel's Grotto for a couple of days to delouse all of our Ariels and all of the wigs, along with the women who maintained the wigs. Studios Ariel shuddered.

Parade Snow White

I saw a young woman who was not in costume for a return-to-work clearance. When cast members were either ill enough or injured enough to be put off duty, they needed to be cleared by a Disney Doc to return to work.

This woman had a pronounced Hispanic accent.

As a matter of course, I asked what she did before I could clear her for duty. She stated she was friends with Snow White in the 3:00 parade.

I later saw this cast member in full costume, wig, and makeup. She looked exactly like Snow White from the animated classic film.

But, she could only be friends with Snow White in the parade. She could never do a meet-and-greet with that accent!

Ariel, a Hero

One day while I was on my rounds, I accompanied a Give Kids the World child to meet Ariel in Ariel's Grotto. This was, in fact, a child with a terminal illness whose wish was to meet Ariel.

Disney princesses meet a quota of at least 172 guests per hour, so they can spend only a few seconds with each guest. The cast members who play princesses are well-schooled at guest interaction and usually handle the time crunch masterfully.

When the guest, her family, and I reached Ariel, I mentioned to Ariel that this child's only wish was to meet her.

Ariel handled it beautifully. She signaled that the line was to stop. She put the child on her lap instead of on the rock next to her. She gave that child all the time the child could ever want.

It's possible that management may have given Ariel points for not meeting her quota that hour. Points are used to punish, and sometimes fire, cast members.

But Ariel earned points of a different kind with me. She gave a poor, terminal child her dying wish. I have a hard time not tearing up as I write about it.

Rash Statements

One of the most common cast member complaints when I was a Disney Doc was rashes from the costumes.

Since the costumes were simply clothes, and the cast members did not normally get rashes from their own clothes, one day I decided to get to the bottom of why so many cast members had rashes on their bottoms—and elsewhere.

In those days, cast members were *never, ever* allowed off property in their costumes. WDW owned three costumes for every cast member: one on their back, one on the rack, and one in the laundry.

Down I went to the tunnel under Kingdom to look at the laundry facility.

What I saw immediately explained the rashes.

In the tunnels were massive industrial-sized washing machines. Running the machines were a few non-English-speaking women who had a never-ending, overwhelming amount of laundry to do. Think about 60,000 cast members putting their costumes into the wash after every shift. The amount of laundry was staggering.

The laundresses had only one way to handle this crushing load. They stuffed as many clothes as possible into the front-loading washers. In fact, they had large sticks that looked like the tampon Civil War cannoneers used to ram powder charges into cannons. The costumes were literally rammed into the washers.

The laundresses then poured an unmeasured, enormous amount of powdered soap into the soap dispensers and waited.

Since dirty laundry arrived unendingly, the loads were all run on the shortest-possible cycle.

There were so many clothes in each washer, and the cycles were so short, I observed that clothes in the center of a machine would come out and not even be wet!

Those "washed" clothes, still dirty and imbued with soap powder, would go on the rack for the next cast member's shift.

I actually saw, on many, many occasions, costumes start to produce soap bubbles if a cast member got caught in the rain.

Today cast members wear their costumes home and launder their own costumes. I have to assume the rash problem has been solved.

I'm Blind!

While assigned to Magic Kingdom, I tried on an example of every fur costume in an effort to discover why there were so many injuries in our fur-wearing cast members.

The answers were easy to understand.

First, the costumes were *heavy*. They not only weighed quite a bit, but they were of multiple layers in order to provide verisimilitude to any guest seeing a character from virtually any angle.

Most had an undergarment that covered the cast member from neck to wrists to ankles.

This was effectively a pair of long underwear, just what one needed on an August day in Orlando. Leggings that included padding, arm coverings with padding, then the actual costume, plus large feet or shoes, usually a skull cap, and finally the head.

Staying hydrated was a major challenge when you sweated *pounds* of fluid while working sets scheduled for thirty minutes on and thirty minutes off.

Heavy heads strained necks with great regularity. Having to animate the character by vigorous head movements added to the neck and shoulder strains.

Then there was the vision problem.

In addition to being a general surgeon, I was trained in the U.S. Air Force as an aerospace medicine physician. One lesson had to do with pilot vision. If the windscreen of an aircraft is a certain distance from the face of the pilot, when the pilot's eye-focus muscles are at rest when looking in the distance, the pilot will automatically focus on the windscreen and any bugs or defects as opposed to seeing what is in the distance. Knowing that vision fact caused USAF aircraft designers never to place a windscreen at that critical distance from the pilot.

When I got into many, many of the fur heads, I found the small, sponge-covered viewing port to be exactly the distance the USAF avoided. The result was that it was natural for the cast to focus on the sponge screen itself instead of looking beyond the screen to see outside.

It took a conscious and continuous effort to focus outside. In some heads, that simply was impossible given the combination of the screen's thickness and color and its distance from the cast member's eyes.

Add to that the small size of the port and the fact that the port was not directly in front of the cast member's eyes, but a distance away, and it was the case that cast members in many fur costumes were nearly blind.

There was no peripheral vision, including downward. So, guests who were anywhere but six feet or more directly in front of the character were invisible.

The fur characters rarely saw the kids—or adults—they were photographed with.

And the characters were vulnerable to anyone beside, behind, or below hitting, tripping, spinning, grabbing, pulling, or vomiting on them.

Fiddling around the SpectroMagic Parade

SpectroMagic was a phenomenal parade and, having been the front end of Slinky Dog in the Studios Toy Story Parade, I was anxious to see what the lighted costumes in SpectroMagic were like.

I met with the parade manager and explained that I could better understand her cast and their injuries if I could experience the parade myself. While I was well known for such odd behavior at Studios, this kind of request was new to the management of Kingdom.

When the manager, Sue, gave me the go-ahead, I appeared backstage on the appointed night. Sue explained to the assembled parade cast who I was and what I was doing there. All were excited to have me try on their costumes.

The one they gave me to try before the parade was Alice. Alice's cast member was a five-foot tall, slight female who had to wear a dress with hundreds of lights, wires, and a cable attached to a car battery. The dress must have weighed between forty and fifty pounds. This girl had to dance and animate for the entire one-plus-mile parade route wearing her heavy costume.

The other costumes were equally lit, wired, and *heavy*.

Sue assigned me to perform Bass Fiddle in the parade. I put on the undergarment, skull cap, sleeves, gloves, and giant shoes, then climbed into the heavy bass fiddle from a hole in the bottom. The costume was suspended on my shoulders by two unpadded metal hooks that dug in directly on my acromioclavicular joints. These joints are notoriously weak in humans and are frequently dislocated.

I danced the parade route in pain. I waved to my wife and kids—I think—because I had given them a particular place to stand. Since I could barely see out of the tiny sponge viewport, the best I could do was recognize where I was in the parade by looking at the third-floor windows on Main Street, U.S.A. When I got to what I thought might be the spot they were supposed to be, I waved. Since I was waving all of the time anyway, that was not really such a feat. Once the parade left Main Street, U.S.A. and went around the hub into Liberty Square, then through Frontierland, I actually had no idea where I was. All I could see was darkness and the tops of trees.

I have no doubt why they gave me Bass Fiddle to experience the parade. The role required no training—just dance and wave. And, the fiddle hurt. A lot. I'm sure Sue wanted me to know that.

I now had a clear understanding of why I saw injuries from this parade. The costumes were heavy and mine, at least, was internally designed very poorly.

My acromioclavicular joints hurt for several *weeks* after doing that parade only once.

Overnight in Kingdom

When the last guest has left the park, and the Kiss Goodnight has been played on the castle, an astounding amount of work is done in Magic Kingdom.

As part of learning all of the jobs, I spent a night with the overnight park manager.

Once the guests were gone, the gates opened and eighteen-wheelers containing merchandise appeared, restocking the shops on Main Street, U.S.A. It was jarring to see these huge trucks driving up and down the street and around the hub.

Now steam cleaners cleaned every sidewalk and street in the Kingdom. Anyone who has ever visited Kingdom knows that the streets are always pristine no matter how much ice cream and soda spills each day. This was explained by the army of cast members that descended at night to pressure wash the streets.

Armorers reloaded fireworks.

Kitchens were made to glisten.

I knew all of these activities were ongoing. What I didn't expect was the overwhelming sound.

Anyone who has visited WDW or worked there is used to the omnipresent background music throughout the property. It is always there, but it is designed to blend in with the atmosphere, to put guests into the magic without being obtrusive. Its absence, replaced by the engines of eighteen-wheelers, forklifts, and steam cleaners was jarring.

Tinker Bell

On some nights and during some fireworks shows, Tinker Bell flies from a castle spire to the roof of the Tomorrowland Terrace Restaurant.

I wanted to see how that worked.

One afternoon, I met with the Tinker Bell manager and an engineer. They took me up the spire of the castle to see where the intrepid cast member playing Tink leaped off.

Tink had a harness that seemed secure when I put it on. Although I had fast-roped from US Air Force helicopters and had skydived, I had to admit that trusting my life to that harness was a little daunting.

However, I was told I was not going to be allowed to fly. The reason had to do with my weight. The tension on the cable was adjusted from the landing spot, and the cable was adjusted to the weight range for the actual Tinks. They were small women. I was neither small nor a woman.

After coming back down from the spire, we went over to the Tomorrowland Terrace roof. Talk about low tech!

The landing spot for Tink is an elevated metal frame. The cable goes over the top of the frame and is attached to heavy metal weights, allowing the cable to flex up and down.

So what did Tinker Bell land into? An old mattress. An old mattress was tacked to the back of the frame. Tink extended her legs straight out and hit the mattress. That was it.

Haunted Mansion

I had so many questions about the Haunted Mansion. After a manager walked me through, I had a few more.

The Haunted Mansion was not originally intended to be a dark ride. Walt had envisioned a walk-through during which guests would have to solve the mystery of the sea captain and his wife. But the reality of throughput changed the plan to the dark ride that is so beloved.

Much of the ride turned out to be standard stuff.

The busts that follow you as you pass are depressed into the wall, not protruding from the wall. That is all that is necessary for the illusion of a turning, following head.

Madame Leota is a projection.

There is an infinity mirror with a scrim and a moving candelabra at the end.

Scrims are used throughout the Mansion. A woven cloth has a painting on one side that is seen when light is shined upon that side. Lighting something behind the scrim causes guests to see what is behind.

The ballroom scene is a Pepper's Ghost (optical illusion).

Walking though these effects was great and allowed me to see how simple the effects, that appear so sophisticated, really are.

The part that was most eye-opening to me, and that caused me more questions than answers, was the behavior of guests while in the attraction.

The manager told me the floor of many of the rooms, including where Madame Leota resides, was covered with pressure sensitive plates that would e-stop the ride if a guest stepped out of their doom buggy. I was told it happened several times each and every day.

Then there were the condoms. Yup, condoms. Haunted Mansion is a dark ride consisting of nine minutes of air-conditioned comfort in a doom buggy that has basically nothing in the way of restraints and is wide enough to accommodate three adult guests. Couples tried so often to have what I would call "a quickie" that there was a special condom patrol at the end of each day. Of course, the condom patrol also picked up any number of other items, including litter, sunglasses, bags of purchased items (that ended up in Cast Connection), etc, etc.

The manager told me that there was an extraordinary number of condoms on the floor of the Haunted Mansion on graduation nights and Nights of Joy. I guess that makes sense.

Security Office

WDW security officers have a virtually impossible job. They are not sworn police, they have no power of arrest, and rely on diplomacy and persuasion to keep peace and order in the parks.

The Kingdom Security Office is down the cul-de-sac off to the right near Crystal Arts when going up Main Street, U.S.A. toward the castle. The office is accessed by going backstage at the end of the cul-de-sac and walking upstairs.

Inside, you find lots of uniformed security officers, and a surprising number of plain-clothes officers writing reports, on break, or preparing to go on stage.

At the time I worked there, prior to 9/11, guests with concealed carry permits could identify themselves at the turnstiles then be escorted to the Security Office to secure their weapon in a safe during their stay.

Shoplifters—and there were plenty of those—found out the Security Office was not part of the magic of WDW.

Animal Kingdom

March of the ARTimals Parade

I had limited exposure to the Animal Kingdom. I spent a few shifts in cast First Aid there, but the number of injuries and occupational illnesses was so low the company could not justify having a Disney Doc there.

Cast members who required more care than one of the nurses could provide were taken by van to either EPCOT or Kingdom First Aid, until Central Health Services opened. Then, all cast with injuries and illnesses were taken by van there.

The March of the ARTimals Parade ran for only fourteen months. The parade debuted in April of 1998 and ended in June of 1999.

There were many problems with the parade. The biggest problem I saw was the width of the pathway around the Animal Kingdom. The path wasn't wide enough for the floats, dancers, and guests. Having to stop and restart the parade was a daily issue as guests were always in the way.

The guests seemed confused and unhappy with the parade. As originally conceived, the parade was about the animals in Animal Kingdom having a party of some kind. The Disney characters were absent. Guests wanted Mickey!

There were tweaks to the parade over the few months it ran, adding some classic characters. But guests were annoyed by the parade as the path around the park simply was too narrow. If they were trying to get anywhere during the parade, they simply could not. Unlike at Kingdom, where there was plenty of room for guests to move even when the parade was directly in front of them, the stopping-and-starting Animal Kingdom parade blocked the entire pathway.

I saw very few injuries from the March of the ARTimals Parade, as the main performers were dancers who were in great physical shape.

But I was glad to see the parade go.

15

Pleasure Island

At the time I was a Disney Doc, WDW converted the Marketplace to Downtown Disney and Pleasure Island. From an economic standpoint, I'm sure this made sense, but I missed the Marketplace.

The Marketplace had been a quiet, relaxed location with a few shops and some wonderful restaurants. It was a great place for lunch and dinner, as well as to pick up merchandise without having to go into the parks. Unlike now, Disney used to have a policy that certain merchandise would be available only in select locations. An example was a grass skirt, which was only available at the Polynesian or the Marketplace.

Conversion to Downtown Disney and Pleasure Island changed all of that.

During the day, guests of all ages could walk between the two venues unimpeded. But after a certain time in the evening, Pleasure Island closed to minors. The dancing and drinking venues there were designed to compete with Church Street in Orlando and City Walk at Universal Studios.

And compete they did.

There was more than one death at Pleasure Island when drunken guests fell into the water and drowned. Further, Security had to deal with the inevitable fights accompanying excessive alcohol use.

I saw only a few patients from Pleasure Island, but they were memorable.

One patient was a young woman who danced on a stage above the guest dance floor. One night she fell off the stage. Her injuries were minor, but she had to be put on some restrictions while her ligament strains healed.

Her description of her working conditions caused me to want to arrange an evening when I could observe the dancers at work. This cast member emphatically asked me not to do so. She said the major reason she did not want me there was that she would be embarrassed to have me see her dancing in a g-string and skimpy top.

I had another dancer, a male this time, with the same injuries and from the same cause as the young woman—falling off of the stage.

Ultimately, Disney converted Pleasure Island and Downtown Disney into Disney Springs. The wild times were over, thank goodness.

In Room

While I was a Disney Doc, WDW signed a supposedly exclusive contract with Florida Hospital to provide house calls to guests in their resort rooms. One other Disney Doc and I were offered the opportunity to move from full-time at WDW back to weekends and become In Room docs.

Those were the days when there was little security at resorts. Anyone could drive onto a resort, something my family and I did regularly, to enjoy dinner at one of the resort restaurants.

We received an In Room car, two cell phones, a set of walkie-talkies, some very *large* and heavy cases with medical supplies and equipment, and a pull cart.

Each doctor was accompanied by a young woman called a PRC. I cannot remember exactly what PRC stood for, but it was something like Patient Registration Clerk.

The doc's job was to drive the car, lift and pull the heavy stuff, and see the patients. The PRC's job was to answer the phones, book appointments, set appointment times, and collect payment for the visits. This was a cash or credit card business—insurance was not accepted.

With their check-in package, guests received a flyer about In Room, should it be needed. The cost was about three times what it cost to go to a walk-in clinic, but many families chose to use the service anyway. Lots of guests did not rent cars, and those who did were not familiar with the area. It was simply easier to spend the money to get service in their rooms.

The job was 24/7, rain or shine. Sometimes it was so busy there was no way anyone could possibly see all of the patients who called. Other times a full day would go by without a call.

The service was discontinued when other doctors and clinics started to do In Room calls, undercutting the price Florida Hospital charged. Since security was so lax at the resorts, Disney simply was not able to keep its part of the "exclusive" access to the rooms agreed to in the contract with Florida Hospital. So Florida Hospital walked.

Stroke

We were called to a room at All-Star Music for a headache. One never knew what to expect when the call was for a headache. Most times it was for a hangover, or for someone seeking a narcotic or opioid prescription. I hated headache calls.

When we got to the room, we found a woman in her forties in bed. Her husband and two adult children and two young children also were in the room.

The room was completely dark with all of the shades drawn and all of the lights out. The husband said she could not stand any light.

She was able to speak but with great difficulty. She said this was the worst headache of her life.

In medical school, we had learned that photophobia (light-causing pain) along with "the worst headache" of someone's life was a subarachnoid hemorrhage until proven otherwise.

A quick physical exam revealed one pupil larger than the other and a distinct weakness on one side of her body.

Clearly, she had suffered a stroke, bleeding deep to the arachnoid membrane. The arachnoid membrane is one of the three membranes that surround the brain and spinal cord, and such a bleed is usually arterial as opposed to venous.

The thing about arterial bleeding is that the arteries have smooth muscle around them, so they will clamp down and slow, or even stop, the bleeding for a while. But when the arterial muscle fatigues, the artery will dilate and the person will bleed extensively—frequently leading to their death or permanent disability.

I called Reedy Creek for an alpha unit, then called the hospital warning them of an impending neurosurgical emergency.

Reedy Creek responded immediately. Usually, the paramedics from Reedy Creek wanted to do their own evaluation which took a considerable amount of time. For once they listened to me and transported the patient without delay.

The patient's family called the next day to say she had been taken to the operating room upon arrival at the hospital, her subarachnoid bleeding artery had been clipped, and she was expected to make a full recovery. It was gratifying to hear them say that my insistence on urgency on the part of Reedy Creek and the ER had saved her life.

An Actual Princess

One morning, very early, we got a call from the concierge to visit a Saudi princess at the Grand Floridian.

A guest services host escorted us to the top floor of the main building. When I say the top floor, that is exactly what I mean. This princess had booked the entire floor of the Grand Floridian's main building.

The rooms on that floor were all multi-room suites, but she needed the entire floor of suites.

Walking down the hall was weird. Sitting or standing, every few feet, were off-duty police officers who worked plain-clothes security for the princess. They stared at us like we were suspected of an assassination attempt at any moment.

When my PRC and I finally got to the end of the hall, we were escorted into a suite that was *much* nicer than anywhere I had ever stayed and much nicer than most places I had ever lived.

In the room were the princess, a small child, and a handful of servants.

I asked the princess what I could do for her. She wanted me to examine the child, who was four or five years old, before she was taken into the park.

The kid had no complaints. She was completely well. But the princess wanted her examined.

Finding nothing wrong, I felt bad charging the exorbitant fee we were required to charge by the contract between Florida Hospital and WDW. She paid without blinking an eye.

Every morning for the next week we received a call from the princess to come and examine the child.

Every morning the kid was fine.

Every morning we charged the fee, and she paid without hesitation.

Because we saw the princess so many times, we got to know her a little. We found out she and her entourage of kids and servants—but *no* males—had flown their private jet to WDW from Saudi Arabia. Their jet was a Boeing 707. A 707 could normally fly up to 174 passengers. Theirs was designed in a private configuration with bedrooms, living rooms, dining rooms, and, I suppose, a few seats.

Because the princess and her entourage were all female, and they were coming to the scary, high-crime USA, they contracted for off-duty officers to discretely protect them 24/7. Of course, the officers had to keep their distance and try not to look at the princess while doing their duty.

Since we were always called to see the princess and her kid first thing in the morning, Disney housekeeping had not been in the rooms yet. It was amazing to me how much of a mess those few people could produce overnight! To say the housekeepers had their jobs cut out for them would be a massive understatement.

I never found anything wrong with the kid I examined every day. By the third day, a second kid was added to the exam roster. The rules between WDW and Florida Hospital said I had to charge full price for each kid. There was never any hesitation to pay.

Each day, the rooms became more and more disorganized as the princess and her people seemed intent on buying *everything* that Disney sold. And, they wanted multiples of each item.

By the last day, entire suites were filled with purchased items. I thought it was a good thing these people had their own 707, an airplane the USAF uses as an aerial refueler because of its massive capability to haul stuff.

On the last day of the visit, when I again found nothing wrong with either of the kids I had examined, the princess presented my PRC and me with gifts.

We were not supposed to take any gratuities.

But she was not presenting us with money. She had bought each of us very expensive items and had them impressively wrapped. She insisted there was no diplomatic way we could refuse.

Not quite knowing how to handle it, I accepted the gifts, instructed the PRC to do the same, and profusely thanked the princess.

I then turned the gifts over to my supervisor at Florida Hospital. I suspect that expensive watch went directly onto the wrist of a hospital vice-president.

Saudi Princes

The Saudi Princess and her retinue were my patients at the Grand Floridian. Both of the Saudi Princes I saw were at different resorts.

The first prince was at the Polynesian. I got a call in the early morning from the Poly concierge to see the prince, and the demand was to get to the resort "immediately." I told the concierge that if the medical need was immediate he should call a Reedy Creek alpha unit. He told me, in no uncertain terms, that the prince did not want an ambulance. But, he wanted to be seen "right now!"

Not breaking any speed laws, my PRC and I got to the room at the Poly in about fifteen minutes.

I didn't know the Poly had rooms like the one we entered.

This prince and his entourage had taken two such rooms. Each room was actually a suite of rooms that covered an entire floor of one of the Poly's guest buildings. This prince took one on both floors of the two-story building.

Reminiscent of the princess at the Grand Floridian, the prince wanted me to examine a boy of eight or nine that had nothing wrong with him. Like the Grand Floridian princess, he called me to see the same kid every day for a week. Also, like the princess, his rooms filled with stuff over the week, so much so that large cardboard cases of Disney merchandise were piled upon each other by the end of his stay.

The second prince had an almost identical story to start with, but his visit ended very differently than the princess or the Poly prince.

This Saudi prince and his aides rented a house. Disney used to have a few houses across Disney Vacation Club Way between the area of the Treehouse Villas and Saratoga Springs. These were complete, large, fully furnished houses for rent.

The week started like the others, with a daily call to see a kid who was not sick.

Two things differentiated this prince and his time at WDW from the others.

The first was that this prince called us twice per day. We made a well-child visit in the morning before they went to the parks and in the afternoon after they returned.

One of the prince's retinue was an older uncle. During one of the afternoon visits, the uncle started to complain of chest pain. He was literally having a heart attack right in front of me.

The prince was adamant that I not call an ambulance. He *demanded*, indeed, he *commanded* me to take care of the uncle right in the house and to involve no one else.

I was equally adamant that the uncle was going to the hospital.

Things got pretty tense for a while, including having to chase the prince and his uncle and the entourage about the house as they moved from room to room trying somehow to convince me that their unreasonable demand would make more sense if I heard it in the kitchen instead of the living room.

I called the ambulance.

The prince and the uncle refused their treatment.

I made it very clear that this was urgent and that the alpha unit had to take the uncle despite his refusal.

Finally, the uncle acquiesced and allowed himself to be carried into the alpha unit. The reason was that his pain became so bad, and his weakness so obvious, it was clear to all and sundry he was going to die.

I never got called back to that house and have no idea if the uncle lived or died.

More Princes

One evening we were called to a room in the Port Orleans French Quarter Resort. The caller identified himself as a Saudi Prince. He said he wanted us to see his child because of an ear problem.

This call was unusual, to say the least. First, it came from the prince himself instead of the concierge. Second, if the prince was really a prince, he would have a staff. Third, I had seen several Saudi princes, none of whom stayed anywhere but the most expensive Disney resorts. Port Orleans is a wonderful, beautiful resort, but it is a moderate resort per Disney's description.

I actually hated going to Port Orleans, both the French Quarter and Riverside. All of the buildings were three stories, and none had elevators. I had to lug the two heavy boxes, with their rolling cart, up and down the stairs, rain or shine.

This call was from a third-floor room. I knew that because Disney resorts all had a unique room numbering system, and after a while, I could tell exactly where every room was in every resort simply by hearing the room number. This room was going to be a fairly long walk, then up three flights. At least it wasn't raining.

When we got to the room, there were three middle-aged men in the room and no child. When I asked, they said the child had gone to bed in the next room of the two-room suite. So, I concluded her ears probably weren't bothering her very much.

The men started elbowing each other, looking from one to the other, and grinning. I was with a PRC who was certain we were one day going to be called to a room to be robbed, and she started acting nervous. Finally the men sat and invited me to sit.

"We want you to write us some prescriptions," the spokesman said.

"What kind of prescriptions?"

All three kept looking from me to the PRC and back again. This particular PRC was an attractive young woman who had once been a flight attendant for a major airline, at a time when flight attendant hiring was at least partially based on appearance.

The spokesman asked if the PRC could leave.

I said that was impossible.

Finally, after much elbowing, grinning, and glancing, the spokesman told me they each wanted prescriptions for 500 Viagra®.

They were not happy when I told them I was not going to write them any Viagra® scripts. We had quite a discussion, bordering on an argument, as they made it clear that I was a hired servant, they were Saudi princes, and I was going to be paid, so "just do it."

I maintained as professional an attitude as I could muster, explained that Viagra® had side effects, that they would each have to have a workup that was absolutely not something I could accomplish during an In Room visit, and that 500 pills each was beyond excessive.

They told me that, although Viagra® cost something like ten dollars a pill in the US at that time, it was much more expensive in Saudi Arabia. They went so far as to try convincing me the only reason they had made the trip to WDW was to buy Viagra®.

I asked them to get the child they had used to lure me to the room, telling them I was charging them for a visit whether I saw the child or not.

From the next room, they produced a young kid who had no complaints. I examined the kid, the PRC gave them the bill and collected their money, and we left.

Not everyone was a satisfied customer.

Not a Good Day at the Beach Club

We received one of the usual "kid with an earache" calls to the Beach Club Resort. I always parked the In Room car in the circle in front of the resort at the direction of the parking attendant cast members.

After examining the patient, we returned to see the car had been the victim of a hit-and-run accident. None of the parking attendant or valet cast members claimed to have seen or heard anything.

I instructed the PRC to tell any callers that we would not be able to get to them anytime soon.

I then called the police and had the valet cast member call Disney Security.

The call I didn't want to make, but did, was to the In Room supervisor at Florida Hospital CentraCare. He was not a pleasant person and had made it clear that I was not on the short list of persons he liked.

He drove to the resort and immediately blamed me for the accident. He wanted to know why I would park where I had parked. He was, in a word, furious.

I assured him I had parked exactly where the cast told me to park, in the exact spot we always parked in at the Beach Club. The PRC and the cast members silently nodded confirmation.

The sheriff arrived, took a report, and, as the car was still drivable, off we went to our next patient.

The mysterious case of the Beach Club hit-and-run was never solved. Amazingly, no cast, despite being right there, saw or heard the accident. Video was not something anyone thought to or possibly cared to ask about.

It was In Room's only accident while I was there, providing 24/7 coverage rain or shine. Oh, well....

17

Celebrities

Part of In Room was seeing celebrities who visited WDW. Celebrities are just people, and they get sick and injured like everyone else.

The fact of the matter, though, was that I sincerely disliked seeing celebrities. I might have known they were just human beings, but sometimes they seemed to have forgotten that fact.

Mr. A's Backdoor Deed

One evening, a concierge called me to the Beach Club Resort. Whenever we got a call from a concierge, we knew there was probably a celebrity or some other high-roller involved.

When we arrived at the room, it was one of the very swanky suites in a portion of the resort not normally visited by the average guest.

The door was opened by a *major* celebrity who had been on *Saturday Night Live* and had gone on to make several major motion pictures.

Sitting on the bed was Mr. A's girlfriend, who, predictably, was something more than gorgeous. She was the patient.

I asked her what I could do for her, and she told me she was bleeding from her rectum.

She was vague about when and how the bleeding started.

However, there were several blood-stained, and a couple of blood-soaked, towels in evidence around the room.

I asked if I could examine her. Sure enough, she had a pretty remarkable anal tear that was clearly fresh but not actively bleeding at the time.

There was nothing I could do for this laceration in the hotel room. Mr. A's girlfriend needed to see someone in the hospital.

Needless to say, Mr. A did not want me to call an ambulance. Since his girlfriend was stable with a normal pulse and blood pressure, and was not actively bleeding, I offered to lead them to the Celebration Hospital with Mr. A following the In Room car.

Believe it or not, Mr. A had the temerity to ask me what might have caused his girlfriend's injury. I had the presence of mind to not say what I was sure had caused the injury. Instead, I discussed a few of the less obvious and less likely causes. This satisfied him that I was not going to rat him out when we got to the hospital, so Mr. A and his girlfriend followed us to the hospital.

I explained what I saw to the ER doctor, and drove away with my PRC.

For some reason, I didn't think Mr. A and his girlfriend would want to take me up on an invitation to our Celebration home for dinner during their stay.

The Twins I and II

I saw The Twins on two different occasions. Sort of…

The first time a concierge called me to The Twins' room at the Grand Floridian, they weren't actually there, despite the fact that the concierge who called us said they were the ones we were to examine and treat.

The room was a spectacular suite with more square footage than my current home.

In the room were The Twins' mother and a younger sister, who would go on to avenge herself later in life.

The mother, a particularly unpleasant individual, said the sister had an earache.

Since most kids, and many adults, have an earache after descending in a pressurized aircraft, I was not surprised.

This young lady was particularly non-communicative. I really could not get her to tell me anything about how she felt. But her mom went on and on about the agony this kid was in.

Frankly, our patient looked like she felt fine.

I examined her, and sure enough, she had a minor earblock that was immediately relieved when I instructed her on how to do a Valsalva maneuver. She held her nostrils closed, took in a breath, then gently forced air up her auditory tubes. I watched her eardrum "pop" and, although the kid still said nothing, I knew her symptoms were resolved.

Still, her mother demanded a prescription for antibiotics. I explained that her daughter did not have an ear infection and did not need antibiotics. I could see no reason to go into the fact that the majority of ear infections in kids were viral and that antibiotics were useless if that was the case.

I ultimately wrote a prescription for an antibiotic and instructed her *not* to fill the prescription unless the symptoms returned. The mom promised to call us back to see the ear again if that happened.

I harbor no illusions that she followed my instructions.

The second time I was called to see The Twins, I actually saw them. I got a call from the clinic manager who had gotten a concierge call. The Twins were "out and about" and could not be bothered either to go to the clinic or return to their Grand Floridian room. The mother was insistent that I see them right away, however. I suggested we meet The Twins at Studios First Aid. After a lot of back and forth among ourselves, the clinic manager, the concierge, and the mom, my suggestion was accepted.

I called Studios First Aid to let them know The Twins would soon arrive via a backstage entrance and requested they be put in a room while my PRC and I drove there.

Thankfully, the Studios nurses were great and accommodated The Twins and their mom.

When I saw them, they both had conjunctivitis. My guess was that they had shared some eye makeup and contaminated each other's eyes.

I tried to make small talk with these two adolescents. They let me know, in no uncertain terms, that speaking to me was beneath them. And Mom was her usual difficult self.

I wrote The Twins two prescriptions and instructed that they not share eye makeup or the medication. They left Studios First Aid by a back door, giving me a final gesture to communicate to me that I was, at best, a servant whom they had blessed with their illustrious presence.

Mr. Branson's Daughter

My PRC and I had just finished a room call at the Boardwalk and were walking through the lobby when we saw an entourage of Disney Guest Services cast members escorting someone who was clearly a celebrity.

I did not recognize him, but he was beaming at everyone and waving to guests, as if they were all fans. This celebrity was enjoying every moment of walking in a public area. Accompanying him were an older woman and a woman who looked to be in her thirties.

I asked the PRC if she knew who that was, and she, like me, did not.

The one thing I was sure of was that this man had had a *lot* of plastic surgery on his face.

We got in the In Room car and had driven no more than five minutes from the Boardwalk when the concierge called us back to say we needed to see Mr. Branson immediately.

Now I knew who he was, and I wished we had received the call before lifting the heavy boxes and carts into the car.

We returned to the Boardwalk and had to be accompanied to a floor I had only been on a few times before. The upper floor of the Boardwalk had suites that were nothing less than upscale full residences. When we entered, Mr. Branson was his smiling self, sitting and talking with the older woman we had seen earlier. He did not get up but did wave to us as we were instructed to immediately examine his daughter.

We were taken through the living room, kitchen, formal dining room, and into a bedroom where the thirty-ish woman was seated.

She began a litany of medical complaints, listing a cornucopia of illnesses she claimed to have, all of which required her to be on massive doses of pain medication.

When I finally got to her actual request, it was clear she only wanted prescriptions for opiates.

At first, she refused but finally decided to allow a cursory exam. That exam, she made clear, would not involve her disrobing in any way. So, after a superficial exam, when I could find nothing acutely wrong with her, I told her I was not going to write her scripts for any opiates.

To say she was unhappy with me and my "horrible attitude" is an understatement.

As my PRC and I left, we walked by Mr. Branson who smiled, waved, and dismissed us without a word.

Ms. Respect

A concierge called us to see Ms. Respect, who was to play that evening at the House of Blues in what is now Disney Springs. She made it clear we were to proceed urgently, as Ms. Respect was in a big hurry to get from her immense suite in the Yacht Club to the HOB.

Ms. Respect had put on a bracelet that had caused a rash on her wrist, and she expected us to relieve her of the rash before showtime.

The concierge also told us to expect the room to be hot, as Ms. Respect never allowed air conditioning in her room when she was going to perform. The concierge went on to say she also did not allow air conditioning in the HOB. This was August in Walt Disney World. It was going to be a hot time in the House of Blues that night.

Fully expecting to find a nickel allergy, and knowing that a steroid cream would help relieve symptoms but would not make the rash magically resolve in a couple of hours, my PRC and I walked the long, long hallways to get to Ms. Respect's suite at the farthest reaches of the Yacht Club.

When we were ten feet from the door, our phone rang. It was the concierge. Ms. Respect changed her mind and did not want to be seen.

Oh, well....

Ms. Daytime Emmy

We got a concierge call to see Ms. Daytime Emmy, who was staying in the same luxury apartment on the top floor of the Boardwalk where we had seen Mr. Branson's daughter.

We were not told what was wrong, but we dutifully trooped to the door with our two large cases on pull carts.

Just as we were about to knock, the concierge called our phone.

Ms. Daytime Emmy changed her mind and no longer wished to be seen.

I never did know what she thought was wrong with her.

Disneyana Convention

My experience with the Disneyana Convention requires some backstory. Disney fans had been holding Disneyana Conventions for several years, but the Walt Disney Company was not involved. Disney was not blind, however, to the amount of money being made on its own merchandise at these conventions. In 1992, Disney hosted its first Disneyana Convention, and continued to hold them until 2002.

Several years before I became a cast member, and while on active duty in the U.S. Air Force, my family and I made one of our many vacation trips to WDW. One of my goals while there was to purchase a Disney trivia book.

I searched the parks and asked cast members, but no trivia book was to be found.

After returning from the vacation, I made enough phone calls to finally reach Dave Smith, the Disney Archivist in Burbank, California. I asked Dave if there was a Disney trivia book that I was just not able to find.

Dave told me there had been such a trivia book several years ago, but that none now existed.

I told Dave it was my intention to write such a book. I described the book I wanted to write as an encyclopedia of Disney trivia, with a short paragraph or two about each entry in the book.

Dave wished me good luck and we rang off.

I started to write. I gathered trivia from wherever I could find it, and there was no shortage of sources.

A couple of years went by while I carefully referenced each and every entry, my book getting longer and longer. I moved from active duty to the Florida Air National Guard, then the Air Force Reserve in Florida, taking up residence in Celebration (see the chapter on Celebration).

Now I had a treasure trove of trivia available to me. My family was in the parks every weekend. I carried a notebook and filled one after another with trivia, all of which went into my growing book.

I carried notebooks when my family went on an inaugural voyage of the *Disney Magic*, having to explain myself to curious cast on both the ship and Castaway Cay. They had never seen someone slowly walking about taking notes before, I suppose.

One afternoon, my wife came into my home office while I was typing away on what had now become a tome.

"I have bad news for you," she said.

She handed me a hardcover book, written by Dave Smith, entitled *Disney A to Z: The Official Encyclopedia Hardcover*. Dave had written the *exact* book I had described to him in our phone call. The format was exactly what I had told him I planned to write.

By this time, I had invested four years in my book. There was so much there, and I didn't want to simply walk away from all of that work. So I decided to change my book to a dictionary.

I changed the format from encyclopedic entries to definitions of the English words as defined or used by Disney.

Changing from an encyclopedia to a dictionary took me two more years, during which time I continued to add to the trivia in my book.

Finally, I felt I had completed my work and looked for a publisher. I sent my book to numerous publishers and was rejected by all of them.

Then I had the brilliant idea to submit to Disney Publishing in New York. I called the editor there and described my book. He said he was excited to see it and asked me to submit it immediately. He went so far as to tell me he was interested in publishing if the writing met his standards.

I submitted my book, along with a cover letter. The cover letter stated my contract as a Disney Doc with WDW included an addendum that this book, in progress when I was hired, was my own property and not the property of the Walt Disney Company.

I got my book back from the publisher with his cover letter. If Disney did not own the book outright then Disney was not interested in publishing it.

So, I self-published. I established a publishing company. I purchased an ISBN number and contracted with a printer. I designed a cover, then a second cover, and had them produced. I bought a bookbinding machine. I went into the publishing business and sent a copy of the book to the Library of Congress.

What I didn't have was the capital to advertise.

I took my book to local bookstores and held book signings. I established a website. I spread the word as best I could to my students—I was an adjunct professor of Anatomy and Physiology at Valencia College while working as a Disney Doc and serving in the Air Force Reserve.

I sold a few books. Not a lot of books, but enough to keep hope alive.

Then the Disneyana Convention was scheduled at the Contemporary Resort. I applied for a booth and paid the exorbitant fee to be a part of the convention. I printed many cases of books.

To get slightly ahead of this story, when the day of the convention arrived I was blown away. People attended from around the world. Guests were dressed in Disney clothing the likes of which I had never seen. One woman wore a sequined denim outfit that was probably worth more than my car.

Booths from around the United States, and the world, had Disney items for sale for ludicrously high prices.

Guests were spending big money for those items.

But back to the opening of the convention.

Disney really did right by me and all the others with booths. They provided tables, drapes, and an extremely attractive banner over each booth.

The clock ticked onto the hour and the doors opened. The first person through the door was Dave Smith!

Dave made a beeline to my booth and purchased a copy. He made no mention of his encyclopedia nor of his stealing my idea.

I have no idea what Dave did with my book. I do know that I was never contacted by the Disney Company for violating any of their copyrights or trademarks. I had been careful to reference each and every one of my entries, giving full credit to Disney for their work.

Soon after the Disneyana Convention, I decided my book was not making enough sales to justify the effort I was putting into selling it.

It went out of print.

Sometime later, I had a student ask me about a book he had found on Amazon. He said he had discovered a copy of *Rizzo's Unofficial Dictionary of the Disney Language* that was on sale for close to 200 dollars. It was autographed by the author, and he wondered if I knew about it.

Yup, I told him. I sure did know. And I was shocked that someone thought my book was worth that much money!

19

Cast Connection

WDW has a lot of merchandise venues. Every attraction ends in one. Every resort has one. There are stand-alones. There are carts. There are a *lot* of merchandise venues.

Quite a bit of merchandise is purchased in excess of WDW's needs.

An amazing number of guests buy something then leave it behind—sometimes right on the counter where they purchased the items!

Some items are not up to Disney quality.

Also, restaurants frequently have excess food that should not go to waste.

Resort furniture gets too worn in appearance to be in a guest room.

A resort decides to renovate.

Costumes are changed for a new style.

What happens to the excess stuff and the used resort furniture?

It goes to Cast Connection!

Cast Connection is actually two shops backstage between the waste treatment plant and the backstage animal area of Animal Kingdom.

The first shop is actually called Cast Connection. It gets clothes, toys, purses, jewelry, groceries, etc, etc, etc. from the parks, resorts, restaurants, and shops. Cast members and their families can purchase this stuff for pennies on the dollar.

The second shop, physically attached to Cast Connection, is Property Control. This is where the furniture, dishes, pots, pans, costumes, gym equipment, TVs, etc. from the resorts and restaurants ends up. Costs here are ridiculously low.

Many cast members do all of their holiday shopping there.

Not everything in Cast Connection is worth buying, however. Recently there were colorful tennis shoes of all sizes. These were in Cast Connection because Disney had purchased the cheapest—in both price and quality—shoes they could find for the dancers in the Kingdom parade. Cast members literally had shoes fall apart while dancing the parade. These shoes were inexpensive, but obviously not worth buying.

I have purchased so much from Cast Connection and Property Control I could not begin to list it all.

A few examples:

My wife's credenza in her office, the coat tree in our entry, a Snow White bird feeder (purchased and left behind by a guest), more clothes for my wife, son, daughters, and grandchildren than can be counted, the majority of our kitchen décor, throws, pillows, purses, wallets, my desk chair, my daughter's TV, filing cabinets, cameras (guests seem to love to leave their cameras behind), so many toys I could fill my own shop, Christmas ornaments—the list goes on and on.

Beautiful Nikon cameras from Photopass when they decided to get new ones.

A prop tree from Snow White's Scary Adventure dark ride—the tree has a face, the branches are arms, and a nailed-on sign says "Turn Back."

My personal favorite is frames. I am an amateur photographer. I have enlarged photos on display at a local airport, two city halls, a local college, and a few museums. All of those photos need to be professionally framed before they can be exhibited.

But I cannot afford professional framing. Fortunately for me, Property Control regularly has pictures that are being replaced in resorts. These pictures are all beautifully and professionally framed. And they usually sell for between one and ten dollars.

I buy them whenever I can. I cut the pictures out of the mats and replace them with my enlarged photos. I have received more compliments on the quality of my frames than I can remember.

All thanks to WDW, Cast Connection, and Property Control.

20

Celebration

Don't get me wrong. I enjoy Disney very much. I worked for them, I go to the parks, I buy their stuff, I watch Disney+, I buy annual passes for my kids, and I have family members who work there now. We are a Disney family.

But living in Celebration underscored the reality of Disney as a business, and a heartless one at that.

In the introduction, I described learning about Celebration, visiting with Charles Adams who was in charge of the project, and becoming involved in helping Charles and his team with ideas. The way Celebration was described when it was in the planning stages sounded like Nirvana.

I changed my entire career, from active duty in the US Air Force to the Guard, then to the Reserve and moved my family to Central Florida just to live in Celebration. And, I had been promised a home site when I made those career and family moves in return for my input in the development of what was to be the hospital—Celebration Health run by Florida Hospital (Now Advent Health).

When we moved to Florida, groundbreaking for Celebration was still one year in the future. We lived in a rented house for one year anticipating a move to Celebration. But Celebration's construction was delayed. Our one-year lease expired, and we moved to a month-to-month apartment.

Not ideal. In fact, far from it.

But Celebration was getting closer and closer to completion, so we made the sacrifice.

Then, with no warning, Charles called to tell me that everything he had promised was no longer the case. I no longer had a guaranteed home site. Disney had decided to hold a lottery for the first eighty home sites in the center of town (where we had been planning to move), for the home sites farther from the center of town, and for places in the planned apartments. Charles gave no explanation for this, other than it was a business decision made by the Company.

On the day of the lottery, Disney treated it like a fair. There were characters, tents for eating and buying merchandise, and for getting information about Celebration. I, and the others like me who had been working on the project, were treated like we were strangers.

My daughter, Joanna, and me at our Celebration homesite.

Amazingly, of the hundreds and hundreds of people who entered the lottery, my family actually won one of the home sites in exactly the location we had planned to move. Coincidence?

To diminish our happiness at our good fortune, we were told Disney had decided to change the value of the home sites and of the homes that were to be built. We had been told that no home in Celebration would be valued above $200,000. We had already been approved for a home loan at that price point. Now, at the lottery, we were told the homes in the city center were to have no cap, and that homes in excess of one million dollars were expected.

So, we had a central city home site, and an approved loan for $200,000, but Disney expected to build a much more expensive home on the property.

Getting the contractor and the home built was its own saga, and belongs in another book.

As we were building the home, we had many decisions to make that Disney made it their business to become involved with.

What color was our home to be? My wife and I, at dinner one evening in the California Grill on the top of the Contemporary Resort, looked at the castle and said, "Those are the colors we want for the house." We envisioned a grey house with a blue tiled roof.

I went to the castle manager and asked what color the grey was so that we could match it. He took me on a tour of the castle and demonstrated that the castle was really multicolored, and only appeared grey from a distance. So my wife and I chose a grey that matched what we thought the castle appeared to be and submitted our wall and roof choices to our contractor.

Not long after that, we received what can only be described as a written summons to meet with someone from Disney at an office building in downtown Celebration. When we arrived, someone we had never met greeted us and said, "You know you cannot have a blue roof."

I took great offense at that statement. I suspected I still lived in the United States and had some freedom of choice.

I was disabused of that notion.

Celebration was a Disney Town, I was told, and Disney dictates what you can or cannot do there. The statement was couched in polite terms, but the message was clear.

The Disney rep then took us to the parking lot of the building, where he had arranged for a roofer to display a massive number of roof models. Disney, in response to our contractor informing on us, had spent heaven-knows-how-much money having model roofs made with the colors and styles of roofs Disney would approve. Each model was at least six feet long and three-to-four feet high and wide. It must have required an 18-wheeler to bring these to the lot that day so that we could choose an approved roof.

When I asked what would happen if we decided on a blue tile roof, I was told, “Then your contractor will not build your house.”

So we chose a different roof.

At the time, on the south side of the EPCOT ball, there was a small lawn that was constantly mowed by a solar-powered automatic mower. I wanted one of those.

I met with the EPCOT groundskeeper to find out about the mower. He told me it was a prototype from a company somewhere, and that he didn’t know how to reach them.

Many phone calls later, I found the company and told them I wanted one of their mowers for my future lawn in Celebration. Although the mower was not yet available for sale to the public, the company agreed to sell me one.

I assume they thought having it run around my lawn would be good publicity for them. The mower required a buried wire at the periphery of the lawn which was powered by a battery that was recharged by a small solar panel. Any interruption of the power to the battery would result in the mower running rampant.

Also, the periphery wires could not be closer than three feet apart or the mower would not go into that area.

When our house was finally built, there was a sidewalk in front of the house and a sidewalk on one side connecting the street to the alley and extending to the next block.

A digression is necessary at this point.

Disney wanted control of Celebration. Residents wanted votes. Those two desires were in opposition to each other. The result was that Disney ceded the town of Celebration to Osceola County so the resident voters could deal with the county for roads, sewage, power, water, etc. But, Disney did not cede all of the town to the county. Disney kept the sidewalks and the crosswalks. Disney foresaw a need to be able to block off streets if some kind of celebration in Celebration was ever to occur. But if the county had the streets, Disney would not have the control they wanted. This convoluted plan required my wife and me to have a second closing on our property, as Disney unilaterally amended every deed when it made the decision about the streets and sidewalks.

Owning the sidewalks and crosswalks solved Disney's control problem. If Disney wanted a street closed, they simply had to block the crosswalks, effectively blocking the streets without having to coordinate with anyone.

That meant Disney owned the sidewalk on the side of our house, which Disney decorated with plants along either side.

Soon after we moved into our house, and with the solar-powered mower cutting away, I came home to find the buried wire on the side of our house dug up and our mower no longer working. I went to the workers who were digging in my yard to find out what was going on.

They told me that Disney not only owned the sidewalk, but two feet on either side of the walk. Disney wanted to widen the walk, so the flowers on either side were being moved two feet out. It was too bad my contractor had not informed us of that fact, as we had paid dearly for landscaping on a two-foot wide strip of Disney property.

Our plants were gone, my wire was destroyed, and I was told in no uncertain terms there was nothing I could do about it.

I re-buried the mower's periphery wire on that side of the house, but, as a result of Disney taking two feet of what I thought was my yard, the wire was now within three feet of itself in one narrow point. So, the mower didn't work anymore.

Then there were the curtains.

My son wanted red curtains in his room. We hung them. Disney went nuts. The stink we stirred up with those red curtains ended up in books and magazine articles about Celebration.

Celebration School was some kind of educational experiment that failed miserably. Our kids were put into neighborhoods as opposed to classes. Kindergarteners through fifth-graders were grouped together, with the idea that the older kids would teach the younger ones. There were two teachers per neighborhood, responsible for somewhere around forty kids ranging in age from five to ten.

What was obvious was the amazing lack of supervision and the poor caliber of teaching that was going on.

In the one year our son and two daughters were in the school they learned nothing. That is not an exaggeration. I had them tested.

One daughter, put in front of a computer and told to research dolphins, ended up writing a paper that stated that dolphins used to live on the land and speak English and had taught the language to humans before the dolphins returned to the sea. She found that information while searching the internet, unsupervised. The teachers didn't even try to correct her!

At the end of the first week of what would have been the kids' second year in Celebration School, we received a call from the school wondering why our son was not attending. Since we had walked him to school each morning, this call was mysterious and very concerning.

I left work and drove to the school, wandering from room to room until I found our son. He had attended each day, but in the wrong neighborhood. Since no one had taken attendance for the first week, no one missed him in his assigned neighborhood and no one noticed him in the wrong one.

We took our kids out of Celebration School that day.

***

It took intensive work to get the kids academically caught up for the wasted year in Celebration School.

As Disney would not allow voting or representation on the part of Celebration residents, the Company assigned a cast member to be the "mayor."

One day I went to see the "mayor" about an issue, one having to do with the many, many promises, all broken, on the part of the company and its relationship to the residents of Celebration.

The "mayor" said since he was leaving, he could tell me "the truth about Celebration."

This is what he told me:

The Walt Disney Company had been requesting a freeway exit from Interstate 4 to World Drive since WDW's inception. The response from the State of Florida was that a freeway interchange would not be built for a private business. So, to get to World Drive from I-4, guests would need to take an exit to US-192 then a second exit to World Drive.

WDW, according to the "mayor," thought it would increase its revenue by two percent per year if there was a direct interchange.

But year after year, the State of Florida refused to build an interchange for a private company.

Until someone at Disney asked the question, "Would you build an interchange if there was a town at the foot of World Drive and near I-4?"

Of course, the state said yes.

So, voila, Disney's Town of Celebration, which Disney abandoned the day the ribbon was cut on the interchange, was now a reality. Disney's Town of Celebration's name was changed to just plain Celebration that day.

All of the sidewalk widening, yard digging, wire breaking, blue roof denying, red curtain screaming, meant nothing because Disney got its interchange and then walked away.

Remember: Disney is a business. And the business of business is to make money.

The Real Magic

The real magic is not the sets, the fireworks, the attractions, the Imagineers, Creative Costuming, the music, or the parking lot tram. The real magic of the Magic Kingdom is the cast. These three vignettes say it all for me:

On two unrelated occasions, I experienced conversations with mothers of Give Kids the World kids who were ending their trips without having filled their character autograph books. Weather, schedules, and the kids' different conditions worked against bringing home that keepsake and memory.

On both occasions I asked to see the books, and they were each pathetic. There were one or two autographs and lots of empty pages.

I asked if I could have the books for a few minutes and took them backstage to one of the zoos. There were always friends of characters on break in any of the zoos. Each time, I explained the situation, and each time the characters' friends *filled* the books. As each cast member is usually friends with more than one character, those books got autographs from a wide range of characters that probably would not have been seen in the parks at all during the guests' visits.

Witnessing the look of gratitude on both mothers' faces was an emotional moment each time.

The third event also had to do with a kid who, for various reasons, was never going to make it to WDW. He sent a Flat Stanley which was given to me, and I was asked to do whatever I could to help make a memory for the kid and his family.

I took Flat Stanley backstage to a zoo that was near Kingdom First Aid, behind the west side of Main Street, U.S.A. When I told the cast what I needed, every one of them, including ones that were on their way out of the door for home, put on a costume. That very large group of characters then went outside and stood on a small backstage rise that was backed by a stand of bamboo. On the other side of that bamboo was one of the curves of the Jungle Cruise. (Yep, the Jungle Cruise is actually right behind Main Street, U.S.A.). The cast posed for an amazing photo holding the Flat Stanley front and center.

The cast makes the magic. The cast is the magic!

If you are not familiar with Give Kids the World, it is a wonderful organization that grants wishes—frequently last wishes—for children and their families suffering from some truly terrible conditions. While I was at Kingdom, I arranged for the leftover cookies from the Main Street Bakery (now the Starbucks location) to be brought to GKTW each evening. It was a small thing that I hope made some kids' lives a little brighter.

Did I Actually Have an Impact?

Did I actually have an impact? I will never know. But there's a chance based upon an executive meeting I was invited to. This was another of those meetings that I, and no Disney Doc, had any business attending. We were invited, and I really don't know why.

The meeting had to do with future plans for Magic Kingdom. There was a lot of talk about Mickey and the rest of the Fab Four, new attractions, new shows, new parades, etc, etc. By now, I had been to enough of these kinds of meetings to know that the majority of the stuff discussed would never happen—or would happen in only a highly modified way.

I cannot remember if they asked my opinion—I doubt it—or if I just decided to open my mouth. But this is what came out:

People bring their kids to WDW to show their kids what the parents loved when the parents were kids. I watched the original ***Mickey Mouse Club*** *on our family's black and white TV. I saw Mickey and Donald and Goofy cartoons in the theater before a feature. I went to Disneyland right after it opened. I know and love the characters, and I bring my kids to the parks to share some of my childhood with them.*

Acknowledgments

To my wife, children, children-in-law, and grandchildren: it's cliche but true--without you I am nothing.

To Jeanne Johansen and Cindy Freeman at High Tide Publications, Inc.: thank you for making an "OK" book so much better!

About the Author

Anthony M. (Tony) Rizzo, M.D. is now a Professor of Anatomy and Physiology at Polk State College in Winter Haven, Florida and has been awarded two endowed teaching chairs. He is twice retired: once from the U.S. Air Force and once from Walt Disney World. Colonel Rizzo was decorated thirty-seven times; his decorations include the National Intelligence Distinguished Service Medal from the Director of National Intelligence, the Intelligence Star from the Director of the CIA, two Defense Superior Service Medals and the Defense Meritorious Service Medal from two Secretaries of Defense.

At WDW Dr. Rizzo was a *Doctor to the Mouse*.

A general surgeon and aerospace medicine physician, in the USAF Dr. Rizzo performed thousands of peacetime and wartime surgeries, deployed to five conflicts, was a chief of hospital services, a chief of surgical services, commanded a 250-bed Aeromedical Staging Squadron, directed the Surgeon General's Think Tank for Homeland Defense, and directed a National Intelligence Center. Dr. Rizzo is a pilot who has flown the F-16B, B-1B, C-130, KC-135, T-37, and the HH-60 helicopter. He now flies his own Velocity aircraft.

Dr. Rizzo has testified in closed session before the House Permanent Select Committee on Intelligence. He was an internationally sought-after speaker while on active duty, speaking on Medical Intelligence, and now speaks regularly around the State of Florida on various flying safety topics.

Dr. Rizzo is the author of *Cheeseburger Pneumonia and Other Surgery Stories* published by High Tide Publications and has authored a number of journal articles including in *Topics in Emergency Medicine* and *The Cortland Forum*, a chapter in the textbook *Aeromedical Evacuation*, and the now long-out-of-print *Rizzo's Unofficial Dictionary of the Disney Language*.

Dr. Rizzo is a woodworker, making everything from pens to furniture pieces. He also turns wands for a magical location at another theme park near WDW. His award-winning photography is currently exhibited in two City Halls, the Winter Haven Airport, a public library, Polk State College, and at the gallery at Theatre Winter Haven. He plays tenor guitar and tenor banjo and has put on multiple solo concerts raising money for homeless families and homeless veterans.

Dr. Rizzo, his wife, and his family are true Disneyphiles who live thirty minutes from the parks in Winter Haven, Florida. Dr. Rizzo is blessed to have his three adult children, their significant others, and his three grandchildren living close by, as they are all in the parks as guests at least once per week!

Other Books by Anthony Rizzo

Sociopaths, Cheeseburgers, and the 'See One, Do One, Teach One' Terror: Brutal Surgical Training of the 70s and 80s

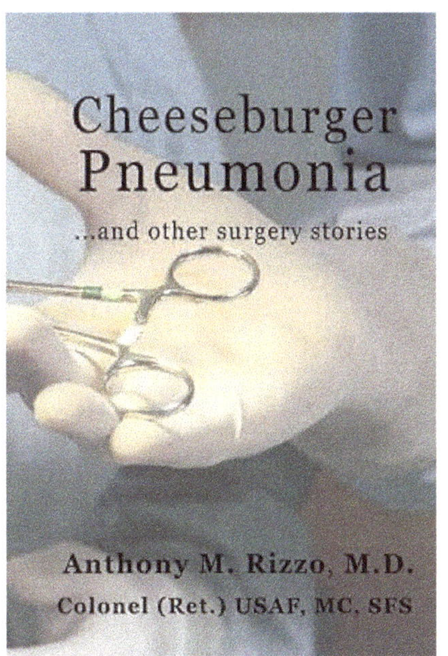

"I wrote this book because the world I trained in has largely vanished. We were improvising at 3:00 AM with limited resources, learning the weight of a scalpel before the internet was there to guide us. It was brutal, it was funny, and it was the making of a surgeon."

Cheeseburger Pneumonia...and other surgery stories offers candid insights into Dr. Anthony Rizzo's experiences during his medical school and residency training in the 1970s and 1980s, as well as his later career as a military and civilian surgeon. Rather than recounting his entire life story, Dr. Rizzo focuses on the unsupervised, often harsh medical training he endured, sharing shocking anecdotes about medical errors, the challenges of working in a male-dominated environment, and the ethical dilemmas he faced while treating patients.

A Message from the Publisher

Stories only truly begin the moment they find their way into a reader's hands.

At High Tide Publications, Inc., we are dedicated to bringing unique voices and unforgettable narratives to life, but that mission is only successful because of you. If this book sparked a new idea, moved you to tears, or simply offered a much-needed escape, your feedback is the most valuable gift you can give to the creative process.

We invite you to share your experience by leaving an honest review online.

In today's literary landscape, reader recommendations are the heartbeat of the industry; they help fellow book lovers navigate the shelves and ensure that talented authors receive the visibility they deserve. Thank you for supporting great storytelling and for helping this book reach its next destination.

My kids don't have the **Mickey Mouse Club** *on TV. There are no Disney cartoons before features in the movies. My kids don't really know who Mickey Mouse is, except for what I tell them and when they see him in the park. My kids have no idea why Mickey is important to WDW.*

But, my kids know Belle, Beast, Ariel, and Hunchback.

When my kids grow up, assuming the parks are still there, they will bring their kids and want to show my grandkids what was important to them when they were little.

So, if you want WDW to continue, you need to stop making more and more plans that are exclusive to Mickey. You need to make plans that include Belle, Ariel, Hunchback, and whatever characters you show to the current generation of children.

If WDW will be a viable thing a generation from now, it can still have Mickey if you tell this generation who Mickey is. But it better have Belle and Ariel and Hunchback or the current generation of kids just won't show up.

The execs looked at me like I had two heads. There was silence in the room. Then they continued the meeting as if I was no longer in the room and as if I had never said a word.

Did I have an impact? As I said, I will never know. But the parks sure have a lot of Belle, Ariel, Lion King, etc, etc, in them....

www.ingramcontent.com/pod-product-compliance
Lightning Source LLC
LaVergne TN
LVHW052354100826
845147LV00013B/841
9781962935746